Photographs courtesy of Anna Saverimuttu; www.id8photography.co.uk; alamy.com

PREFACE

Around £1 billion per year is spent on measures to prevent and deal with homelessness. The social costs of homelessness are significant and would be even greater without this public expenditure. In its most visible form, a relatively small number of people may be roofless and living on the streets. But there are many more that live in emergency and temporary accommodation which can have harmful consequences for their health, employment and other prospects.

There are a number of different measures of homelessness and varying trends within those measures. Rough sleeping has reduced dramatically in recent years. After increasing up until 2003, the number of people seeking and receiving help from councils under the homelessness legislation fell during 2004. But the number of households placed in temporary accommodation under the homelessness legislation has continued to grow. The availability of affordable housing has fallen in many parts of the country. Effort and additional investment is being made in order to increase the supply of housing, and this may help alleviate future pressures. But homelessness cannot be tackled effectively by simply building more houses. The challenge is to find more effective ways of dealing with the wider causes of homelessness and to prevent it wherever possible – to tackle homelessness as a symptom of social exclusion, not just of lack of a roof.

This report examines the work of the Homelessness and Housing Support Directorate within the Office of the Deputy Prime Minister. The Directorate employs targeted funding, specialist advice and objective setting to ensure that homelessness is tackled more effectively within central government and by the local authorities that have front-line responsibility for the homeless and voluntary sector agencies who provide services to homeless people.

The Directorate has a number of priority areas for improved performance. It has encouraged more responsive and co-ordinated approaches to homelessness from local authorities and other agencies, to prevent people becoming homeless in the first place. In addition it oversees two targets which address the most extreme forms of homelessness – reducing the numbers sleeping rough and preventing lengthy stays for families with children in Bed & Breakfast accommodation.

We have found that:

- The Directorate's target setting, combined with directed financial support and advice, has helped to bring about significant achievements. The amount of rough sleeping is less than one third of the levels of six years ago. Up to 24,000 families with children have enjoyed improved surroundings whilst waiting for a permanent home as a result of achieving the target to reduce the number of families with children in Bed & Breakfast accommodation.

- Local authorities have successfully innovated and developed new approaches. For example, by using alternatives to Bed & Breakfast accommodation many local authorities have released savings to improve other services to the homeless. We estimate that achieving the Bed & Breakfast target produced annual savings of up to £50 million for local authorities. However, continuing achievement of targets requires sustained effort.

- Considerable progress has been made in developing and supporting more co-ordinated responses locally and nationally. A new statutory requirement on local authorities to develop a homelessness strategy has raised the profile of homelessness services and encouraged a new emphasis on prevention.

- For further progress to be made, the Directorate should pursue vigorously more reliable and more sophisticated data on the causes and patterns of homelessness, and evidence on the cost-effectiveness of different preventive approaches.

EXECUTIVE SUMMARY

Background

1   When the term "homeless" is used, many people have an image of a person sleeping rough in a cardboard box on a city high street. In fact, the vast majority of people recorded in official homelessness statistics are living with friends or relatives, or have been helped to find temporary accommodation until a settled home becomes available.

2   There are 20 million households in England, of which more than a million move home each year. Most of these move in a constructive and organised way. However, the circumstances of a relatively small but significant number of others put them at risk of homelessness, for example where relationships or families break down, when they are struggling with debt, suffer traumatic events or mental health problems, develop substance dependency or are affected by other personal problems and can no longer keep the home they rent or own **(Figure 1)**.

3   Around £1 billion per year is spent on measures to prevent and deal with homelessness, covering Bed & Breakfast, leased and hostel accommodation, general administration and other related costs **(Figure 2)**.

4   Homelessness can have a profound impact on the health, welfare and employment prospects of those who experience it. One study has suggested that the life expectancy of rough sleepers is only 42 years.[1] Other studies suggest that children in insecure or temporary accommodation often have their schooling disrupted. They may not have space to play or do their homework and are more prone to behavioural problems. They may also suffer from a poor diet where they are forced to share cooking facilities.

5   A key structural factor in the level of homelessness is the supply of affordable housing. In some parts of the country demand has pushed prices up beyond the reach of a significant proportion of the population, thereby increasing pressure on the rented sector. The amount of new social housing has declined in recent years. There is a large backlog of households in shared dwellings and those in various forms of temporary or unsatisfactory accommodation who are all in need of inexpensive, secure housing.

6   The research for this report on the Government's progress in tackling homelessness was undertaken before the publication of the Office of the Deputy Prime Minister's (OPDM's) five year plan "Sustainable Communities: Homes for All," published in January 2005. This plan sets out a strategy for increasing housing supply, affordability and quality, reducing homelessness and halving the number of households in insecure temporary accommodation by 2010. Additional funding to increase the supply of new social rented housing and to expand preventive services is part of a package of measures intended to reduce homelessness.

7   Homelessness is caused by more than housing problems. The challenge has been to find more effective ways of dealing with homelessness problems as they arise and to develop sound approaches to help prevent homelessness wherever possible. "Homes for All" contains more details of work in progress and proposed to support effective prevention as part of the Government's overall strategy to reduce homelessness.

1   Grenier P (1996) Still dying for a home, Crisis.

1 How families and individuals can become homeless

Family homelessness

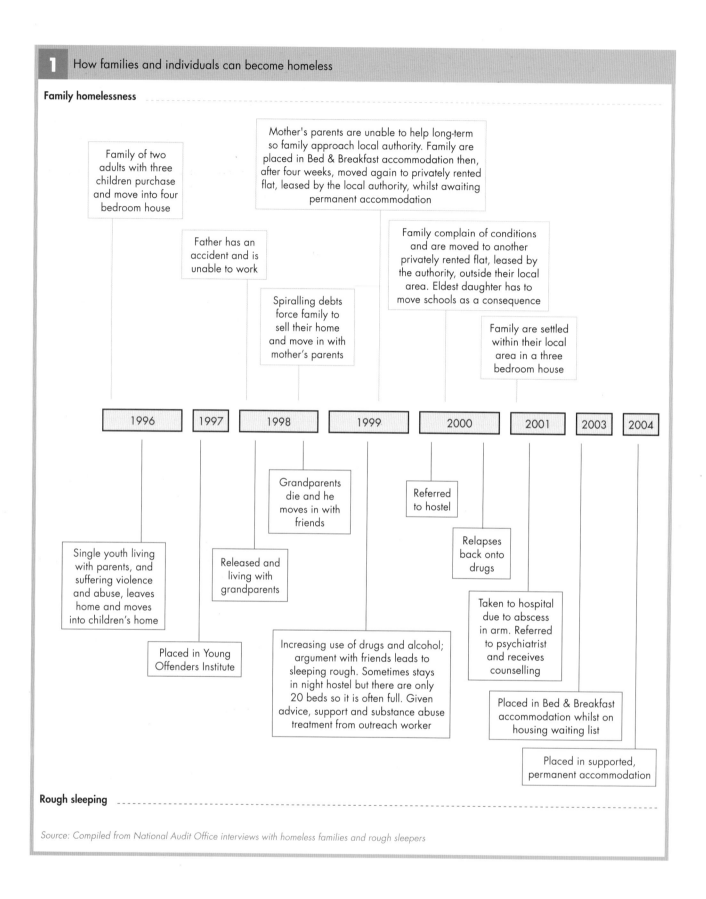

| Family of two adults with three children purchase and move into four bedroom house | | Mother's parents are unable to help long-term so family approach local authority. Family are placed in Bed & Breakfast accommodation then, after four weeks, moved again to privately rented flat, leased by the local authority, whilst awaiting permanent accommodation |

Father has an accident and is unable to work

Family complain of conditions and are moved to another privately rented flat, leased by the authority, outside their local area. Eldest daughter has to move schools as a consequence

Spiralling debts force family to sell their home and move in with mother's parents

Family are settled within their local area in a three bedroom house

| 1996 | 1997 | 1998 | 1999 | 2000 | 2001 | 2003 | 2004 |

Grandparents die and he moves in with friends

Referred to hostel

Relapses back onto drugs

Single youth living with parents, and suffering violence and abuse, leaves home and moves into children's home

Released and living with grandparents

Taken to hospital due to abscess in arm. Referred to psychiatrist and receives counselling

Placed in Young Offenders Institute

Increasing use of drugs and alcohol; argument with friends leads to sleeping rough. Sometimes stays in night hostel but there are only 20 beds so it is often full. Given advice, support and substance abuse treatment from outreach worker

Placed in Bed & Breakfast accommodation whilst on housing waiting list

Placed in supported, permanent accommodation

Rough sleeping

Source: Compiled from National Audit Office interviews with homeless families and rough sleepers

2 The nation spends around £1 billion a year to prevent and deal with homelessness[1]	
	£ million
Office of the Deputy Prime Minister	
Grants to local authorities and voluntary and community sector	60
Supporting People funding for those who have been homeless or are at risk of it	350
Capital funding (via Housing Corporation Approved Development Programme)[2]	24
Local authorities	
Hostel accommodation (gross)	62
Bed & Breakfast accommodation (gross)	270
Leasehold accommodation (gross)	78
Administration and welfare costs	93
Other costs	66
Less grants from the Office of the Deputy Prime Minister (included in line 1)	(45)
Total	**958**

Source: National Audit Office/CIPFA

NOTES

1 This figure does not show wider savings in public expenditure arising from the above funding streams.

2 The needs of the homeless are integrated into other Housing Corporation funding streams.

How homelessness is tackled

8   Front-line responsibility for helping homeless people find a home falls to local authorities. They have a statutory duty to house those who are homeless and in "priority need". Priority need groups include households with children, those who are vulnerable as a result of age, disability or poor health, and people fleeing violence – these are the "statutorily homeless". Local authorities have a range of other duties and powers, for example to review homelessness and produce a strategy at least every five years. They also must provide free advice on homelessness prevention to anyone in their area. Additionally, many people find their own solutions or turn to the voluntary and community sector to meet their housing and support needs, without needing to engage with a local authority.

9   Where permanent social housing is in short supply, or the homeless household needs extensive support, local authorities use "temporary accommodation" to house those to whom they have a statutory duty. In some cases, this may take the form of Bed & Breakfast hotels, hostels or refuges. More commonly, authorities use privately rented or leased properties, or social housing units. In many cases, they also work in partnership with voluntary and community sector bodies, which provide housing and care for both the statutory and non-statutory homeless.

10   The use of temporary accommodation to house those found to be statutorily homeless has risen dramatically in recent years – from around 40,000 in 1997 to over 100,000 by September 2004. The use of temporary accommodation tends to be concentrated in those parts of the country with greater general housing supply pressure. Around 60 per cent of those who occupy temporary accommodation are in London. Around 19 households per 1,000 in the capital are occupying some form of temporary accommodation.

The scale and spread of homelessness

11   Analyses produced by the Barker Review of Housing Supply[2] have estimated that over 400,000 households are in urgent need of secure, affordable and self-contained housing.

12   The number of households presenting themselves as homeless to local authorities rose from 242,000 in 1997 to 300,000 in 2003, an increase of 24 per cent. The numbers that local authorities accepted as unintentionally homeless and in priority need of accommodation increased from around 100,000 in 1997 to 137,000 in 2003 – a 37 per cent rise. Some of this rise reflects a widening since 2002 of the categories of vulnerable groups for whom local authorities must secure housing.

13   During 2004, the number of applications and acceptances fell in each of the first three quarters. If this trend were to continue, we might expect the figures for the whole year to be around seven per cent lower than in 2003 – that is to say around 280,000 applications and 127,000 acceptances.

14 London has the highest numbers of homeless households, both in absolute terms, and in relation to population density **(Figure 3)**. Yorkshire & the Humber and the North East also have high levels of homelessness in relation to population density although they are not subject to the same level of housing pressure as London. The South East and East of England have the lowest rates of acceptances relative to population.

3 In absolute terms, and in relation to population levels, London had the highest number of households accepted as homeless and in priority need in 2003

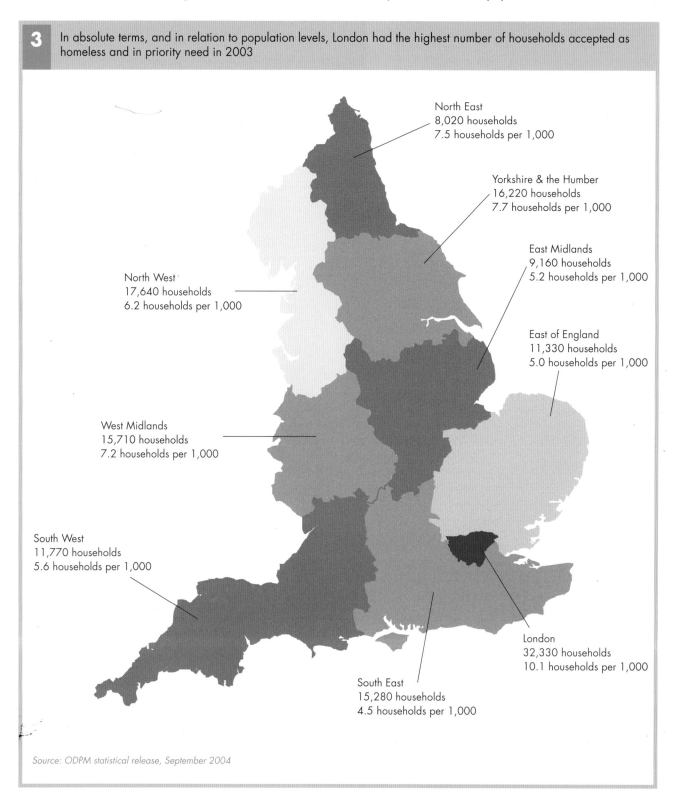

North East
8,020 households
7.5 households per 1,000

Yorkshire & the Humber
16,220 households
7.7 households per 1,000

East Midlands
9,160 households
5.2 households per 1,000

North West
17,640 households
6.2 households per 1,000

East of England
11,330 households
5.0 households per 1,000

West Midlands
15,710 households
7.2 households per 1,000

South West
11,770 households
5.6 households per 1,000

London
32,330 households
10.1 households per 1,000

South East
15,280 households
4.5 households per 1,000

Source: ODPM statistical release, September 2004

A new approach to homelessness

15 In March 2002 the Government published "More Than A Roof"[3], which established the need for a new and more coordinated approach to tackling homelessness. It declared that homelessness was closely associated with social exclusion, and highlighted the need for coordinated action over a period of years. It also urged the development of services that would help people before they find themselves in a crisis situation. In addition, the Homelessness Act 2002 placed new duties on local authorities including the requirement to develop and publish strategies for dealing with homelessness **(Figure 4)**.

16 The Government has established targets relating to two of the most extreme manifestations of homelessness. They address the exposure of children to Bed & Breakfast accommodation, which is often of a poor standard and may involve sharing facilities, and the level of rough sleeping. The targets are:

- **that by March 2004, local authorities will ensure that no homeless family with children has to live in a Bed & Breakfast hotel, except in an emergency, and even then for no longer than for six weeks** (set in March 2002); and

- **to sustain levels of rough sleeping that are two-thirds below the levels recorded in 1998, or lower** (a target to achieve this reduction was set in July 1998, and a target to sustain or improve on the reduction was set in 2002).

17 A separate Homelessness Directorate within the ODPM was established in 2002. In 2003 it merged with the Housing Care and Support Division to form the Homelessness and Housing Support Directorate ("the Directorate"). Its role is to:

- promote homelessness prevention **(Figure 5)** and the effective implementation of the Homelessness Act 2002;

- reduce the inappropriate use of Bed & Breakfast accommodation for homeless families with children;

- reduce the numbers of people sleeping rough;

- develop approaches to tackling homelessness which result from constructive working across departments; and

- deliver a programme providing housing related support for vulnerable groups, known as "Supporting People".

---

4 The main provisions of the Homelessness Act 2002

A strategic approach

Local authorities had to carry out a multi-agency homelessness review and develop a strategy for their area to prevent homelessness, by July 2003.

Additional powers to assist the homeless

The Act gives local authorities the freedom to secure housing for homeless households who are **not** in priority need, allowing them to help people in their community.

Strengthening the duty local authorities owe to the homeless

Local authorities must now secure housing for unintentionally homeless households in priority need for as long as it takes to find a settled home, rather than for just two years.

Extending local authorities' duty-to-house to more vulnerable people

An Order increased the categories of vulnerable groups for whom local authorities must secure housing. Local authorities must now house a wider range of unintentionally homeless people, including those who are:

- vulnerable as a result of fleeing domestic, racial or other forms of violence

- vulnerable as a result of an institutionalised background in care, the Armed Forces or prison

- 16 and 17 year olds whose support networks have broken down irrevocably and who are not owed a duty by social services.

Source: National Audit Office/HMSO

NOTE

The Act received Royal Assent on 26 February 2002 and applies to England and Wales.

---

3   ODPM (2002), More than a Roof. Online at http://www.odpm.gov.uk/stellent/groups/odpm_homelessness/documents/page/odpm_home_601520.hcsp

5	How homelessness can be prevented

Cause	Action
Parents, relatives or friends not being able or willing to provide accommodation	Mediation services, usually contracted out by local authority to, for example, Relate
Relationship breakdown, including domestic violence	'Sanctuary' schemes, which allow domestic violence victims to remain in their homes once security measures are in place
End of assured shorthold tenancy	Housing advice. Rent deposit or bond schemes to encourage landlords to let to potentially homeless people. Landlord-tenant mediation services, to resolve disputes about behaviour or repairs
Mortgage and rent arrears	Debt counselling. Advocacy services in magistrates' court. Fast tracking housing benefit claims
Person ill-equipped to sustain a tenancy	Advice and support under the Supporting People programme for vulnerable people at risk of homelessness, for example improving budgeting and 'life' skills
Lack of information	Early and proactive intervention from local authority homelessness services to discuss options and offer assistance and advice

Source: National Audit Office

18 In 2004-05, the Directorate allocated just under £60 million to local authorities and a range of voluntary and community sector bodies to promote improved practices in preventing homelessness and improving the lives of those who experience homelessness **(Figure 6)**. Additionally, in 2004-05, the Directorate is distributing Supporting People funds of over £350 million, part of a wider £1.8 billion programme. These funds are designed to help authorities plan, commission and provide housing related support services specifically to help vulnerable people who have been homeless rebuild their lives and help those at risk of homelessness to sustain independent living in their own homes.

The focus of this report

19 After considering the scale and nature of homelessness in England (Part 1), we examined progress towards the Government's two key targets and the impact they have had (Part 2). We also evaluated the progress in encouraging new approaches to tackling homelessness (Part 3).

20 We surveyed over 200 providers of homelessness services, visited six local authorities, interviewed people who were (or had been) homeless, consulted with a wide range of bodies, convened a panel of homelessness experts to guide our work, examined ODPM's independent evaluation of local authority homelessness strategies[4] and analysed available sources of homelessness statistics. Our methodology is explained in more detail in Appendix A.

---

4   HQNS (2004), Evaluation of Local Authorities' Homelessness Strategies, ODPM.

6 The delivery chain – the role of key national, regional and local bodies in tackling homelessness

1 Homelessness and Housing Support Directorate (ODPM)

- Sets policy and targets

- Conducts overall financial management and monitors performance

- Gives specialist advice and collates and spreads best practice

- Works in partnership with other central government departments

- Oversees the Supporting People programme – housing related support to vulnerable people

9 Government Offices in the Regions

- Develop government programmes at regional and local level

- Support the local authorities in their area

- Work in partnership with local organisations and local people

354 Local Authorities

- Assess homeless applications

- Give advice and other help to prevent homelessness

- Hold the statutory duty to house those in priority need and homeless

- Conduct homelessness reviews and develop homelessness strategies

- Work in partnership with the voluntary and community sector and housing providers

- Allocate temporary and permanent accommodation using their own social housing stock, privately rented/leased accommodation and Registered Social Landlords

500+ Voluntary and Community Sector organisations

- House statutory and non-statutory homeless people, for example in hostels for rough sleepers

- Offer advice, support and treatment for substance abuse and other issues

- Give training, skills and development such as workshops and courses

2000+ Registered Social Landlords

- House statutory and non-statutory homeless people nominated by local authorities

- Supply and manage temporary accommodation under contract to local authorities

- Provide supported accommodation and ongoing tenancy support

- Build and let new social housing

- Manage 1.45 million homes across England

Source: National Audit Office

FINDINGS

In relation to the Bed & Breakfast target

"That, by March 2004, local authorities will ensure that no homeless family with children has to live in a Bed & Breakfast hotel, except in an emergency, and even then for no longer than six weeks"

21   We estimate that as a result of the setting of the target up to 24,000 families with children have so far experienced improved surroundings and quality of life whilst waiting for a permanent home. Aside from a small number of special cases, the target was met by the intended date of March 2004. When the target was set two years earlier, local authorities were accommodating some 7,000 families in Bed & Breakfast hotels of which 4,000 had been resident for six weeks or more.

22   The initiative represents good value for money by successfully "investing to save". Progress has been achieved through careful targeting of special funds by the Directorate on those local authorities who faced the biggest challenges in meeting the target, for example by switching to use of better forms of accommodation. Bed & Breakfast accommodation is an expensive option, and longer term arrangements with private sector landlords can prove to be much cheaper. We estimate that national annual savings to local authorities could be as much as £40-50 million.

23   Wider benefits for homeless people have arisen as a result of the setting of the target. The approaches used to move families out of Bed & Breakfast hotels are equally applicable to other homeless people in Bed & Breakfast accommodation. Many authorities are using the resulting savings to re-house other client groups in better forms of temporary accommodation, or to address other homelessness priorities.

24   After the target date, there was a slight increase in the number of families with children in Bed & Breakfast accommodation for more than six weeks, although the Directorate informed us that their latest monitoring (ahead of formal data on the quarter ending December 2004) shows the number to have fallen again. A small number of families are likely to remain for more than six weeks, reflecting exemptions allowed in the new legislation applying from 1 April 2004 which gives the target a statutory basis. It is important that such use is confined to exceptional cases, and does not re-emerge as a significant problem.

25   The quality of alternative accommodation to Bed & Breakfast is still variable. Whilst in general temporary accommodation alternatives to Bed & Breakfast hotels offer better surroundings, especially for children, the quality is variable. The Directorate has consulted on new minimum standards, which are to be included in revised statutory guidance.

In relation to the rough sleeping target

"To sustain levels of rough sleeping that are two-thirds below the levels recorded in 1998, or lower"

26   The national target reduction in rough sleeping has been met and sustained. Local authorities produce official data on rough sleepers by making an annual count or an estimate of people sleeping on the street. In 1998 there were 1,850 rough sleepers in England on a single night. The recorded number of rough sleepers fell by over 70 per cent between 1998 and 2004 to just over 500.

27   The setting of the target combined with financial support and advice from the Directorate has helped to stimulate new local approaches to tackle rough sleeping. Vulnerable adults are now better identified and supported by homelessness services. Local authorities have established more co-ordinated approaches and worked in closer partnership with voluntary and community sector partners as well as with health and addiction services to improve services to rough sleepers.

28   The fall in rough sleeping in London has not been as great as the fall nationally. Half of all people sleeping rough in England do so on the streets of London, and particularly in Westminster. The numbers in London have fallen significantly since 1998, but not by as much as two-thirds.

29   There is a lack of robust information on the sufficiency of accommodation to help house and support former rough sleepers. Since rough sleepers often have complex problems, they are particularly likely to fall into a pattern of repeat homelessness. They therefore need a programme of support to address their initial problems, and access to suitable accommodation (often referred to as "move-on" accommodation) to help their rehabilitation back into normal life. But there is a lack of definitive evidence as to whether there is sufficient "move-on" accommodation of the right type that can be matched with the right type of support service, especially in London.

Encouraging new approaches nationally

30   The bringing together of a number of former units dealing with separate aspects of homelessness and housing support into a single Directorate has helped to develop a more co-ordinated approach to homelessness issues within ODPM. It has also helped to provide a focal point for homelessness policy more widely within central government.

31   Through its engagement with a range of central government departments and agencies, the Directorate has helped to achieve a number of changes in policies and procedures and sponsored a number of promising initiatives. These have brought about, or have the potential to bring about, improvements in the services provided to homeless people; in particular, by working with:

- the Prison Service to ensure that prisoners' housing needs are identified, and to help prisoners sustain their existing accommodation on entry to custody or find permanent accommodation on release. This work has included supporting the provision of housing advice centres in prisons;

- the Home Office to encourage schemes which allow the victims of domestic violence to stay in their original homes;

- the Department of Health to help address the health needs of rough sleepers and those in temporary accommodation;

- the Ministry of Defence to establish schemes to provide advice and shelter for ex-service personnel; and

- the Department for Education and Skills on pilot schemes to provide respite care, emergency accommodation and support for young people who have run away from home or who are at risk of being expelled from the family home.

32   While the Directorate has made progress in widening the data collected, there remains a need for further hard quantitative data to inform national policy development and implementation on a number of issues. Local authorities still collect only very basic information (using P1E forms) on the causes of homelessness. The P1E is designed to monitor the decisions and actions of local authorities under the homelessness legislation, rather than to provide detailed information on homeless households. This form of data collection limits our understanding of homelessness in England, and of the scale and nature of interventions required. A major survey of 2,500 homeless households has been commissioned by the Directorate for 2005, which is intended to improve the evidence-base for its policies. A review of the statistics on homelessness has also been announced in "Homes for All".

33   Tackling homelessness strategically as a symptom of social exclusion, not just of lack of a roof, is complex and multi-faceted. The Directorate has embarked on a number of pilot projects, research programmes and evaluations across a wide field of issues and in collaboration with a number of different agencies. The lessons from this work, as well as that carried out by the voluntary sector, need to be brought together and analysed so that priorities can be set to build on the success in reducing the scale of rough sleeping and use of Bed & Breakfast accommodation. For example the Directorate has commissioned an evaluation of homelessness prevention work which may help achieve this. We found that the expertise of the Directorate and the quality of its support was well-regarded by local providers of services to the homeless but that they would welcome a lead on where their future priorities should lie. "Homes for All" provides this lead, setting a challenging new aim to halve the number of households in insecure temporary accommodation by 2010.

34   The Directorate needs to work further with the National Asylum Support Service (NASS) and the Housing Corporation to make the most of opportunities to secure housing for the homeless.

- NASS makes use of leased accommodation to house asylum seekers whilst their request for asylum is being assessed, but its current contract arrangements with landlords do not provide for this accommodation to be used by local authorities to house the homeless. With the recent reductions in asylum applications, some of this property is under-utilised, and NASS is closing down some contracts with providers. The Directorate and NASS are working together to make better use of empty NASS properties and need to establish whether the under-utilised properties are in the right locations to be used to provide temporary accommodation for homeless households.

- In an increasing number of areas, local authority housing departments retain strategic responsibility for meeting housing need but social housing is provided and managed by Registered Social Landlords (housing associations) or Arm's Length Management Organisations. Some local authorities told us that Registered Social Landlords at times refuse to house individual homeless households (which are often economically inactive and may require support to sustain their tenancy) and the Directorate has recently published good practice guidance to help improve cooperation in this area. There is a lack of hard evidence on how real or widespread is the problem of Registered Social Landlords acting unreasonably or failing to meet the regulatory requirements placed upon them.

Developing services locally

35   The statutory requirement to review local services to the homeless and develop a strategy by July 2003 has raised the priority that local authorities and other agencies give to homelessness services. The great majority of local authorities believe the requirement to produce a strategy in combination with the setting of targets has raised the profile of homelessness issues and the need to tackle them. The majority of community and voluntary sector bodies working with the homeless agree. In the localities we visited the profile had been raised not just amongst local authority staff but more widely amongst public service agencies and local politicians.

36   There has been increased liaison between local authorities, the voluntary and community sector and other public sector agencies in planning for homelessness services. Many disparate services are in contact with homeless people or those at risk of it in any one local authority area. Basic co-ordination of services is vital to enable sharing of information to target need and avoid duplication. We found that the requirement to draw up a strategy had helped to strengthen local partnerships.

37   In drawing up strategies, local authorities have reconsidered how best to approach homelessness in their area. Many local authorities have identified potential new and novel approaches in their strategies. Some have used targeted central funding to restructure their services. Around 85 per cent have placed a new emphasis on preventing homelessness.

38   The homelessness strategies of many local authorities do not set out specific and measurable ways in which their intentions are to be turned into reality and concrete improvements in services brought about. An evaluation commissioned by the Directorate found that very few authorities had set themselves 'SMART' objectives (specific, measurable, achievable, relevant, and time-related) in their first strategies, although many authorities have been required to do so, as a condition of their grant funding. Many local authorities have not identified the resources required for their plans. Some authorities have developed homelessness fora, which have a role in monitoring the strategy and flagging up areas of concern, but more could be done to involve the full range of service users in shaping service development.

39   Some local authorities would have benefited from earlier feedback on their strategies, although the Directorate told us that this would have been difficult to achieve in practice. While all authorities received formal feedback from the Directorate in Summer 2004, some authorities completed an early review of progress without the benefit of being able to address common issues identified by the Directorate.

40   Systems to collect and spread good practice in the provision of services to homeless people could be improved, and are currently over-reliant on local and informal networks. More could be done to identify and spread good practice in the provision of services to the homeless. There is little definitive evidence about what works cost-effectively, and preventive efforts are particularly difficult to evaluate. The Directorate's current evaluation and proposed good practice guide on prevention should address this.

41   The nature and extent of regional bodies' role in tackling homelessness is varied. Government Offices in the regions have a potentially important role in ensuring local solutions take account of regional issues. We found differences in their approaches, for example in the amount of assistance that they give to local authorities, and the extent to which homelessness is reflected in regional housing strategies.

RECOMMENDATIONS

42 The Homelessness and Housing Support Directorate has made good progress in improving the effectiveness of services for homeless people. To help ensure further progress is made, we make the following recommendations.

To strengthen its strategic role the Directorate should:

a **Develop a timetabled plan for improving data on the causes, patterns and nature of homelessness and repeat homelessness.** Collecting such data is not easy given the sporadic and fragmented nature of contact by many of the homeless with service providers. But the evidence gap hinders effective identification of priorities. Local authorities have identified difficulties over data availability as an issue where further guidance would be welcome in developing homelessness reviews and strategies.

b **Be clearer about the outputs and outcomes it expects from its liaison with other central government bodies.** The Directorate is engaged with a wide range of departments and agencies across government, but needs to clarify the outcomes to be achieved from this work.

c **Disseminate cost-effective strategies for preventing homelessness.** While many local authorities have devised homeless prevention schemes, they would welcome more shared knowledge about what works well and which schemes offer best value for money. The Directorate has commissioned an evaluation of best practice, and should ensure that it is properly disseminated perhaps by sponsoring a dedicated website for practitioners.

d **Clarify the Government Offices' role.** At present, they are taking different approaches and providing varying levels of assistance to local authorities. The Directorate therefore needs to be clear about what it expects from the Government Offices' involvement.

To build on the success of the achievement of targets the Directorate should:

e **Set out in the new homelessness code of guidance the minimum standards expected for temporary accommodation, and evaluate whether these standards are met.** Since the quality is variable, local authorities and households placed in temporary accommodation need to be given clearer guidance about minimum acceptable standards.

f **Encourage local authorities to extract the lessons learnt from moving families out of Bed & Breakfast accommodation, and apply them to other groups in temporary accommodation.** The Directorate has had considerable success in using targeted funding and offering specialist advice to help local authorities move families with children out of Bed & Breakfast hotels. Some local authorities have used this opportunity to re-evaluate their provision of temporary accommodation to other priority need groups.

g **Establish the extent of problems in accessing move-on accommodation for former rough sleepers and other hostel residents.** More needs to be done to ensure that the route from hostel to settled accommodation is as efficient as possible.

To further promote more co-ordinated approaches the Directorate should:

h **Establish whether there is hard evidence that Registered Social Landlords are failing to meet the statutory and regulatory obligations placed upon them to co-operate with local authorities in providing accommodation for homeless households.** Some local authorities believe that Registered Social Landlords are able to avoid these obligations, and that nomination agreements, which are designed to reserve a fair share of housing for homeless people and others in housing need, could be made clearer and more enforceable.

i **Work with the Home Office's National Asylum Support Service (NASS) to identify whether there are under-utilised NASS properties, of the right type and in the right places, to house homeless people.** Existing NASS contracts preclude the use of leased accommodation for any group apart from asylum seekers. The Directorate should take forward its planned project with NASS to explore opportunities for more flexible use of empty asylum accommodation where this is appropriate and cost-effective.

National Asylum Support Service

j **The National Asylum Support Service should develop a system to promote better case working and information exchange with local authorities.** This would allow local authorities to better estimate demand, and work more closely with NASS and other landlords to make provision for former asylum seekers given Leave to Remain in the UK, so that they do not have to make homelessness applications in the first place.

Department of Health

k **The Department of Health should nominate a lead officer with responsibility for co-ordinating work on homelessness issues to provide a central reference point for homelessness.** Despite various pieces of work being taken forward, in general, liaison on health issues could be improved.

ANNEX
The case study areas

Carlisle

The historic city of Carlisle is located in the County of Cumbria close to the English/Scottish border. Carlisle is mixed in terms of disadvantage, being ranked as 108th most deprived district out of 354 nationally. Carlisle is a relatively prosperous city with an unemployment rate of 2.6 per cent (claimant count March 2003) lower than the regional (3.6) and the national rate (3.0).

Carlisle has no recorded rough sleepers and had not used Bed & Breakfast as temporary accommodation until Spring 2004.

In 2001 15 per cent of households in Carlisle rented from the Council but in 2002 the City Council transferred its housing to Carlisle Housing Association. It retained two hostels providing temporary accommodation for the homeless.

- **The John Street Hostel** is a direct access hostel providing short to medium term accommodation for 21 single men.

  Eight 'satellite' houses are linked to John Street providing home share accommodation for a further 24 men.

  The Hostel works in partnership with the statutory sector and voluntary agencies to ensure that the necessary support is available for hostel residents to enable them to deal with any personal problems associated with homelessness and social exclusion.

  A resettlement service is provided which assists residents to move on from hostel to permanent accommodation.

- **The London Road Hostel** is short term accommodation provided for women and families while their homeless applications are assessed. The Hostel can accommodate up to 10 households of varying size.

  The hostel residents are provided with advice and support during their stay in the hostel and there is close liaison with other statutory and voluntary agencies in the provision of support services.

  Following the assessment of their homeless applications residents may move into permanent tenancies with Registered Social Landlords or into other forms of housing.

Sources: ODPM, Census 2001, Carlisle Council Website http://www.carlisle.gov.uk/carlislecc/main.asp?page=211

Total Number of Households: **43,963**

Government Office: **North West**

House Price Index August 2004: **22.7**[5] (Base Feb 2002)

Population 100,739

Employed 45,359

Unemployed 2,584

Retired 11,590

Other 41,206

Rented: Council 15.3%

Rented: Registered Social Landlord 3.0%

Privately rented 10.8%

Owner occupied 70.9%

5 HOUSE PRICE INDEX - August 2004. ODPM calculates a monthly house price index that covers purchases for owner-occupation and for buy-to-let. The higher the price index, the higher the rise in house prices.

Statistics	June 2002	September 2004
Accepted as being homeless and in priority need	6	69
Number per 1,000 households	0.1	1.6
Households in Temporary Accommodation	6	48
Hostels	0	48
LA/HA Stock	6	0
Private Sector	0	0
Bed & Breakfast	0	0
Other	0	0

NOTE

Care should be taken when comparing statistics for the June and September quarters in any year because of seasonal variations in homelessness.

Rough Sleepers (June 1998)   0

Rough Sleepers (June 2004)   0

Homeless Directorate Funding: Recommended Allocation 2004-05: £28,000

Doncaster

Doncaster Metropolitan Borough Council is in the heart of the former coalfields, and geographically is the largest Metropolitan Borough in the country. Doncaster is quite deprived being ranked 40th most deprived district out of 354 nationally.

Temporary Accommodation is provided via Supported Housing Schemes:

- **M25 Housing**

  Direct Access Hostel. Thirteen bed space Night Shelter access is available from 9.00 pm to 8.30 am and a charge of £1.00 is made for the night.

  Seventeen bed space hostel (12 male and 5 female beds).

  Four bed spaces shared accommodation for single people aged 18 or over. The maximum length of stay is 6 months.

  Five bed spaces for homeless people 45 years or over. The maximum length of stay is 6 months.

- **Doncaster Women's Aid Refuge**. Accommodation with support for women and children who are fleeing domestic violence.

- **Doncaster Foyer**. Forty bed spaces for young single people between the ages of 16 and 25. Length of stay up to 2 years.

- **YMCA**. Wood Street 26 bed-sits for young people aged 18 to 25.

- **DHYP**. The Young Women's Housing Project provides accommodation for vulnerable young women aged 16 to 25.

- **Stonham Housing**. Eight bed spaces for single males.

- **Stonham Supported Housing Scheme**. Ten properties are leased by the Council to Stonham Housing Association.

- **South Yorkshire Housing Association**. Five bed spaces with support for young, single care leavers (length of stay up to 2 years).

Sources: ODPM, Census 2001, Doncaster Homelessness Review

Total Number of Households:
118,699

Government Office:
Yorkshire & the Humber

House Price Index
August 2004:
25.1
(Base Feb 2002)

Population
286,866

Employed
115,415

Unemployed
8,662

Retired
31,415

Other
131,374

Rented: Council
19.1%

Rented: Registered Social Landlord
1.8%

Privately rented
9.5%

Owner occupied
69.6%

Statistics	June 2002	September 2004
Accepted as being homeless and in priority need	13	47
Number per 1,000 households	0.1	0.4
Households in Temporary Accommodation	64	10
Hostels	0	1
LA/HA Stock	60	9
Private Sector	0	0
Bed & Breakfast	2	0
Other	2	0

NOTE

Care should be taken when comparing statistics for the June and September quarters in any year because of seasonal variations in homelessness.

Rough Sleepers (June 1998)   8

Rough Sleepers (June 2004)   0

Homeless Directorate Funding: Recommended Allocation 2004-05: £80,000

Hammersmith & Fulham

Hammersmith & Fulham is a London borough of contrasts, with economic opportunity and significant pockets of deprivation. The borough has a high unemployment rate of 4.0 per cent (claimant count average 2003) compared to the London average (3.6) and national rate (3.0).

The rented accommodation market within the borough consists of 16,000 privately rented properties, 14,000 council properties and 11,000 Registered Social Landlord properties.

The council managed to reduce the use of Bed & Breakfast accommodation principally by approaching private landlords to provide temporary accommodation. As at 30 September 2004 (see below) in addition to 1,779 units of temporary accommodation, the borough used 3,800 units of supported accommodation provided by the voluntary sector.

Sources: ODPM, Census 2001, Hammersmith Homelessness Strategy

Total Number of Households:
75,438

Government Office:
London

House Price Index August 2004:
6.5
(Base Feb 2002)

Population
165,242

Employed
80,753

Unemployed
6,447

Retired
10,038

Other
68,004

Rented: Council
19.2%

Rented: Registered Social Landlord
13.5%

Privately rented
23.4%

Owner occupied
44.0%

Statistics	June 2002	September 2004
Accepted as being homeless and in priority need	142	141
Number per 1,000 households	1.8	1.7
Households in Temporary Accommodation	1,530	1,779
Hostels	141	12
LA/HA Stock	266	420
Private Sector	532	1,229
Bed & Breakfast	591	118
Other	0	0

NOTE

Care should be taken when comparing statistics for the June and September quarters in any year because of seasonal variations in homelessness.

Rough Sleepers (June 1998)   11

Rough Sleepers (June 2004)   4

Homeless Directorate Funding: Recommended Allocation 2004-05: £1,500,000

Lambeth

Lambeth is a diverse London borough with larger than average population from a multitude of backgrounds with a variety of needs. Over 40 percent of Lambeth's households live in social rented housing, far higher than the London average. The borough has one of the highest unemployment rates at 5.6 per cent compared to the London average (3.6) and national rate (3.0).

The Council managed to reduce its dependency on Bed & Breakfast accommodation by introducing more private sector leasing arrangements. The council provided landlords with incentives such as risk free, long term leases, usually 3 to 5 years with no management/agency fees. They have developed a wide range of approaches to providing temporary accommodation:

- **Lambeth owned hostels** are used for people who are made homeless at very short notice.

- **Lettings First, Private Sector Leasing** a partnership formed with Avenue Lettings, part of the Amicus Housing Group, to help acquire private rented sector properties for use as temporary accommodation.

- **Private Agents Sub-Leasing Scheme.** Private sector leasing where properties are leased to the Council through a selected number of private agents.

- **Homeless Initiative Leasing.** This is a new partnership between Lambeth Housing and London and Quadrant Housing Trust (LQHT) for the provision of up to 80 good quality self-contained properties for use as temporary accommodation for the homeless.

- **Guinness Trust.** The Council set up a scheme with Guinness Trust in August 2002, for nominations to properties owned and managed by them for use as temporary accommodation.

- **Licensed Temporary Accommodation.** These are one-bedroom Council properties let on licence to single parents with a child under 5 or pregnant women.

- **Short-Life.** Lambeth uses a small number of empty properties earmarked for redevelopment or disposal.

- **Bed & Breakfast (Shared Accommodation).** The Council has significantly reduced its dependence on the use of shared B&B for families with children and only now places priority single homeless people in Bed & Breakfast.

- **Bed & Breakfast (Self-contained).** Some households are placed in self-contained hotel annexes.

Sources: ODPM, Census 2001, Lambeth Homelessness Review & Lambeth Council Homelessness Website
http://www.lambeth.gov.uk/servdir/cgi-bin/nph_ld.exe?SectionDetailHXBCA

Total Number of Households:
118,447

Government Office:
London

House Price Index
August 2004:
6.5
(Base Feb 2002)

Population
266,169

Employed
125,800

Unemployed
12,368

Retired
14,714

Other
113,287

Rented: Council
28.5%

Rented: Registered Social Landlord
12.8%

Privately rented
21.5%

Owner occupied
37.2%

Statistics	June 2002	September 2004
Accepted as being homeless and in priority need	402	306
Number per 1,000 households	3.1	2.3
Households in Temporary Accommodation	1,802	2,077
Hostels	301	299
LA/HA Stock	737	48
Private Sector	33	1,183
Bed & Breakfast	451	303
Other	280	244

NOTE

Care should be taken when comparing statistics for the June and September quarters in any year because of seasonal variations in homelessness.

Rough Sleepers (June 1998)   20

Rough Sleepers (June 2004)   12

Homeless Directorate Funding: Recommended Allocation 2004-05: £2,000,000

Manchester

The city has undergone significant economic and physical regeneration over the last six years; it has some of the most deprived wards in the country and is ranked 2nd in the index of deprivation 2004. The unemployment rate, at 5.4 per cent, is higher than the national average (3.0).

Manchester achieved the Bed & Breakfast target by leasing private sector properties; changing its allocation and nomination policy for permanent accommodation; supporting private sector tenancies better and increasing the emphasis on prevention and advice services.

The council manages approximately 54,000 homes and employs 305 people in the homelessness division. Manchester has access to a range of temporary accommodation:

- **Men's Direct Access Centre.** Applicants accommodated: single men, childless couples. The centre has 33 single rooms, one of which is adapted for an elderly or disabled person.

- **Women's Direct Access Centre.** Applicants accommodated: single women, childless lesbian couples. Accommodation, staffing and facilities are similar to the men's direct access centre.

- **Woodward Court.** Applicants accommodated: single men and women, childless couples. Woodward Court has 60 self-contained flats in a converted multi-storey block.

- **Young Persons Shared Houses.** Applicants accommodated: single men and women (16+). Each house is single sex with eleven single occupancy rooms. There are four houses for men and one for women.

- **Shared Houses.** Applicants accommodated: single men and women (aged 16+). There are 15 houses, each accommodating between 10 and 15 residents, throughout Manchester.

- **Homeless Families Shared Temporary Accommodation.** Manchester Housing has properties providing temporary accommodation for homeless families and pregnant women in a shared environment. They provide a total of 113 bed spaces; rooms are of various sizes.

- **Homeless Families Temporary Accommodation.** (Self-contained scheme) Applicants accommodated: families and pregnant women. The scheme currently consists of 250 furnished council properties throughout the city.

Sources: ODPM, Census 2001, Manchester City Council Website
http://www.manchester.gov.uk/housing/strategy/homeless/review/tempacc.htm

Total Number of
Households:
167,451

Government Office:
North West

House Price Index
August 2004:
22.7
(Base Feb 2002)

Population
392,819

Employed
132,145

Unemployed
14,316

Retired
29,185

Other
217,173

Rented: Council
28.6%

**Rented: Registered
Social Landlord**
10.8%

Privately rented
18.8%

Owner occupied
41.8%

Statistics	June 2002	September 2004
Accepted as being homeless and in priority need	570	343
Number per 1,000 households	3.1	2.0
Households in Temporary Accommodation	562	727
Hostels	140	194
LA/HA Stock	245	364
Private Sector	0	0
Bed & Breakfast	57	69
Other	120	100

NOTE

Care should be taken when comparing statistics for the June and September quarters in any year because of seasonal variations in homelessness.

Rough Sleepers (June 1998)   31

Rough Sleepers (June 2004)   18

Homeless Directorate Funding: Recommended Allocation 2004-05: £767,000

West Wiltshire

West Wiltshire is a largely rural district in South West England and is divided into 43 parishes and includes the market towns of Trowbridge, Melksham, Bradford upon Avon, Warminster and Westbury. West Wiltshire has a very low unemployment rate of 1.4 per cent (claimant count average 2003) – lower than the regional (2.0) and national rates (3.0). West Wiltshire homelessness review found that there has been a significant growth in the number of homeless applicants who are both young and vulnerable or who are vulnerable because of mental health needs.

As at April 2002 West Wiltshire had the following mix of housing:

■ 86.25 per cent of all housing was provided in the private sector;

■ 12.5 per cent of housing was provided by Registered Social Landlords;

■ 1.25 per cent of housing was provided by the public sector – mainly the Ministry Of Defence.

West Wiltshire District Council does not manage any permanent housing itself, having transferred its housing stock to West Wiltshire Housing Society (approximately 7,000 homes) between November 1996 and March 2001. The Council does however own and directly manage three hostels (66 units) which are used as temporary accommodation for homeless households:

■ Hillside, Warminster;

■ Ethandune, Trowbridge;

■ Kingsbury Square, Melksham.

When the Bed & Breakfast target was introduced in March 2002, the council approached Sarsen Housing Association to provide temporary accommodation through Private Sector Leasing Schemes.

Sources: ODPM, Census 2001, West Wiltshire Homelessness Strategy & Review

Total Number of Households:
49,407

Government Office:
South West

House Price Index
August 2004:
12.7
(Base Feb 2002)

Population
118,150

Employed
56,134

Unemployed
1,900

Retired
12,325

Other
47,791

Rented: Council
1.8%

Rented: Registered Social Landlord
10.2%

Privately rented
11.1%

Owner occupied
76.9%

Statistics	June 2002	September 2004
Accepted as being homeless and in priority need	68	42
Number per 1,000 households	1.4	0.8
Households in Temporary Accommodation	120	155
Hostels	59	55
LA/HA Stock	0	4
Private Sector	14	76
Bed & Breakfast	30	3
Other	17	17

NOTE

Care should be taken when comparing statistics for the June and September quarters in any year because of seasonal variations in homelessness.

Rough Sleepers (June 1998)　　　0

Rough Sleepers (June 2004)　　　0

Homeless Directorate Funding: Recommended Allocation 2004-05: £78,000

PART ONE
Arrangements for tackling homelessness in England

"As the number of homeless people continues to rise, a more strategic approach needs to be developed, not only to address the symptoms, but to tackle the causes too"[6]

Tackling homelessness as a symptom of social exclusion is complex

1.1 When the term "homeless" is used, many people have an image of a person sleeping rough in a cardboard box on a city high street. In fact the vast majority of people recorded in official homelessness statistics are living with friends or relatives, or have been helped into settled or temporary accommodation.

1.2 There are 20 million households in England, of which more than a million move home each year. Most of these move in a constructive and organised way. However the circumstances of a relatively small but significant number of others puts them at risk of homelessness, for example where relationships or families break down, where they are struggling with debt, suffer traumatic events or mental health problems, develop substance dependency or are affected by other personal problems and can no longer keep the home they rent or own.

1.3 Homelessness can have significant negative consequences for the people who experience it. At a social level, rising levels of homelessness have an impact on social cohesiveness and economic participation. At a personal level, homelessness can have a profound impact on health, education and employment prospects. For example:

- life expectancy among rough sleepers is 42 years, compared to the national average of around 74 years;[7]

- homeless children in Bed & Breakfast accommodation are exposed to a higher risk of accidents or catching infectious diseases. Their school attendance is often disrupted, and they are more prone to behavioural problems such as aggression[8]; and

- largely excluded from the labour market, homeless people rely on benefits for their main source of income. Since most temporary accommodation is expensive, and is normally funded through Housing Benefit, they may feel they are in a benefits trap that acts as a disincentive to work.

1.4 In many cases homelessness is a symptom of underlying personal problems. Having a settled place to live is likely to be insufficient. A coordinated package of support – relating to health, education, benefits and other issues – may be needed if the person is to find a sustainable solution to homelessness.

Housing supply will continue to be a factor

1.5 Homelessness is inevitably influenced by the availability of housing, and particularly affordable housing. Of England's 20 million households, around 3.9 million (19 per cent) live in social housing.[9] The Barker Review of Housing Supply,[10] published in 2004, noted that the number of social houses built in the United Kingdom fell from around 42,700 per year in 1994-95 to around 21,000 in 2002-03. It also found that, while there had been a considerable increase in spending on social housing (from £800 million in 2001-02 to over £1.4 billion in 2003-04), rising land prices and the need to improve existing stock meant that the rate of new supply had continued to decline. The Review concluded that the number of new social and affordable houses would have to rise by at least 17,000 per year, requiring expenditure of up to £1.2 billion, in order to meet the flow of new needy households.

1.6 The Barker Review also highlighted the considerable number of households in need of affordable housing. It is suggested that over 400,000 households are in need of self-contained, secure and affordable accommodation in England alone **(Figure 7)**.

7	There are over 400,000 households in need of self-contained housing in England	
		'000
Households in temporary accommodation		94
Households in "stop gap" accommodation, i.e. staying with family or friends		154
Households in shared dwellings		53
Single homeless people, hostel residents, etc		110
Total		**411**

Source: Delivering Stability: Securing our Future Housing Needs, Kate Barker, 2004

---

6   "More Than A Roof", Office of the Deputy Prime Minister, 2002.
7   Crisis, Annual Report 2003-04.
8   "Living in Limbo" – survey of homeless households in temporary accommodation, Shelter, June 2004.
9   Survey of English Housing 2003-04, National Centre for Social Research.
10   Delivering Stability: Securing our Future Housing Needs, Kate Barker, March 2004.

1.7 While the Spending Review 2004 included plans to build an extra 75,000 social rented homes, almost 70,000 households purchased their home under the Right-to-Buy legislation in 2003-04 alone. Many of these households would have stayed in their home regardless, and so there is little impact on the supply of social housing. But the Barker Review estimated that the sub-market sector will lose the capacity to re-let around 22,000 properties per year as a result of Right-to-Buy.

1.8 Housing pressures are likely to continue at least into the medium term. The challenge, therefore, has been to find more effective ways of dealing with homelessness problems as they arise, and to develop a sound, evidence-based approach to prevention.

Local authorities have a statutory responsibility to house people who meet specific criteria

1.9 Front-line responsibility for helping homeless people falls to local authorities. The Housing (Homeless Persons) Act 1977 set out their responsibilities. The concept of "statutory homelessness" is used by some people to define those in priority need of housing. The 1977 Act has since been amended, most notably by the Housing Act 1996 and the Homelessness Act 2002. Priority need groups were widened in 2002 and now include households with children, 16 and 17 year-olds, those who are vulnerable as a result of age (old or young), institutionalisation, disability or poor health, and people fleeing violence.

1.10 The statutory responsibilities of the local authority depend on the applicant's circumstances. The local authority does not have to house those who are not homeless, or those who are homeless but have no priority need for accommodation. The local authority must, however, make advice freely available to all. It may choose to accommodate those to whom it has no statutory duty, or give them other help. The households themselves have a number of choices. Many seek help from the voluntary and community sector, and are housed for the short-term in hostels or shelters. Others stay where they are, or go to stay with family or friends. A very small number may resort to sleeping rough on the streets.

1.11 Local authorities can only assess a person's housing status and take the necessary action if that person approaches them for assistance. Many have to move but are able to help themselves, perhaps with the aid of family and friends or voluntary and community organisations. Some though are not organised or aware enough of local authorities' services, or simply do not want statutory help.

The withdrawal of supportive relationships is a significant cause of homelessness

1.12 At a national level, reliable data are held only on those who are accepted as unintentionally homeless and in priority need. Among this group, over one-third lost their last settled home because parents, relatives or friends were no longer willing or able to provide accommodation. A further 20 per cent lost their home due to the breakdown of relationships, most of whom had experienced domestic violence **(Figure 8)**. However, only the two most recent or pressing causes of homelessness are recorded. The data may therefore not reflect the underlying cause of homelessness.

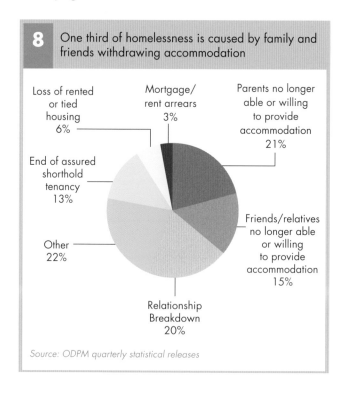

8 One third of homelessness is caused by family and friends withdrawing accommodation

Loss of rented or tied housing 6%

Mortgage/ rent arrears 3%

Parents no longer able or willing to provide accommodation 21%

End of assured shorthold tenancy 13%

Other 22%

Friends/relatives no longer able or willing to provide accommodation 15%

Relationship Breakdown 20%

Source: ODPM quarterly statistical releases

1.13 For many people, homelessness is a one-off event. But others can find themselves in a cycle of social or financial difficulty which leaves them without a settled home on several occasions. Since 1 April 2004, local authorities have been required to identify cases of repeat statutory homelessness. It is therefore difficult to ascertain the trend in the level of repeat homelessness across the country. ODPM have analysed local authority estimates that suggest, on average, around ten per cent of those accepted as homeless and in priority need may have been statutorily homeless before. A Scottish study[11], on a different basis, found a repeat homelessness rate of 27 per cent.

The number of people accepted by local authorities as being homeless and in priority need rose sharply between 1997 and 2003

1.14 In 2003, local authorities made decisions in over 300,000 cases where households sought assistance under the homelessness legislation. They accepted just over 137,000 as being unintentionally homeless and in priority need in 2003 compared to just over 100,000 in 1997 **(Figure 9)**. In part, these increases have resulted from the widening of priority need categories in 2002. Just over half of those accepted are in priority need of accommodation because they are families with dependent children, and an additional ten per cent include a pregnant woman.[12]

1.15 The number of applications and acceptances has however fallen slightly, quarter on quarter, since September 2003. The number of acceptances in the quarter ending September 2004 was 11 per cent lower than the same quarter in 2003. (30,600 compared with 34,710).

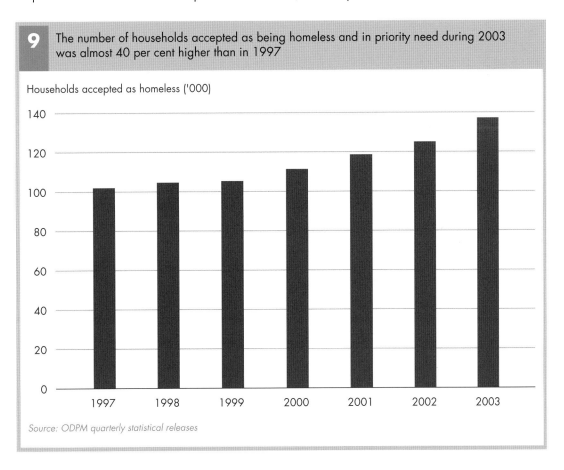

9 The number of households accepted as being homeless and in priority need during 2003 was almost 40 per cent higher than in 1997

Households accepted as homeless ('000)

Source: ODPM quarterly statistical releases

11   Pawson H, Third H and Tate J (2001), Repeat Homelessness in Scotland, Scottish Homes.
12   ODPM Quarterly Statistical Releases.

1.16 London has the highest numbers of households accepted by local authorities as statutorily homeless, both in absolute terms, and in relation to population density (Figure 3, page 6). But there are significant numbers in most major cities, and pockets of homelessness also occur in rural areas **(Figure 10)**. Yorkshire & the Humber and the North East also have high levels of homelessness in relation to population density although they are not subject to the same level of housing pressure as London. The South East and East of England have the lowest rates of acceptances relative to population.

The use of temporary accommodation has dramatically increased

1.17 Some local authorities are able to quickly place people who make successful homeless applications in settled social housing. However, just under half the households accepted as unintentionally homeless and in priority need are placed in some form of temporary accommodation. This term comprises many types of housing unit, such as:

- Bed & Breakfast hotels (seven per cent);
- hostels or women's refuges (twelve per cent);
- homes rented from the private sector (51 per cent);
- homes provided by Registered Social Landlords (six per cent); and
- local authority "council" housing set aside for the purpose (22 per cent).

1.18 The number of households in temporary accommodation increased by almost two and a half times between 1997 and 2004 – from around 40,000 to over 100,000 **(Figure 11)**. Most of the increase has been in the use of self-contained homes rented from the private sector.

1.19 Before the 2002 Homelessness Act the duty on local authorities to provide accommodation for statutorily homeless households lasted for two years. Local authorities now have a duty to secure accommodation until settled housing can be found, or the duty is brought to an end by the household in some other way. Hence the term "temporary" is potentially misleading. While around a quarter of the households who are provided with a settled housing solution spend little time in temporary accommodation, some households find themselves in temporary accommodation for many years.

10 Rural homelessness

When most people think of homelessness, they draw a mental picture of a rough sleeper in an urban setting. But in two of our case studies (Carlisle and West Wiltshire), we found that rural homelessness has a different pattern requiring a difference in response. Although there are few, if any, rough sleepers, rural areas suffer:

- **Housing pressure.** The chance of finding accommodation in the home village may be small. If accepted as homeless, a household is more likely to be placed away from health, education and social support networks. As a result the small towns have to accommodate a disproportionate number of homeless people.

- **Difficulties in delivering services.** Potentially homeless people in rural areas may be more dispersed across the district. This makes publicising services more complicated. They may also lack easy transport – some services like tenancy support have to be taken to service users.

Source: National Audit Office

1.20 The use of temporary accommodation tends to be concentrated in those parts of the country with greater general housing supply pressures **(Figure 12 on page 34)**. Around 61,000 of England's 100,000 households in temporary accommodation are in London.

Establishing the Homelessness and Housing Support Directorate within ODPM represents a new approach to tackling homelessness

The organisation of the Directorate

1.21 A Homelessness Directorate within ODPM was established in March 2002. It brought together the former Rough Sleepers Unit, the Bed & Breakfast Unit (which dealt with issues surrounding the use of Bed & Breakfast hotels as temporary accommodation) and a new homelessness team responsible for implementing the homelessness legislation and helping local authorities to develop their new strategies. This coincided with the publication of "More Than A Roof", which set out the basis of a new approach to tackling homelessness. It declared that homelessness was a manifestation of social exclusion, and highlighted the need for coordinated action over a period of years. It also urged the development of services that would help people before they find themselves in a crisis situation.

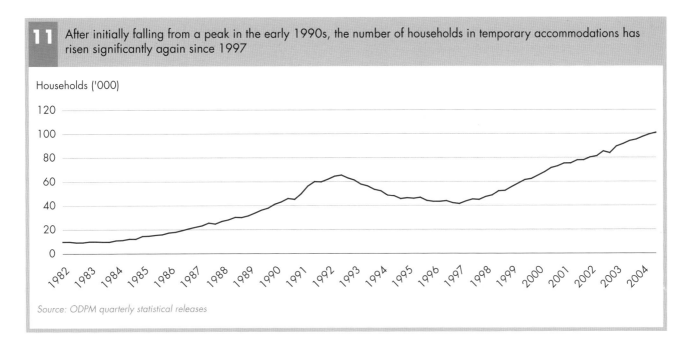

11 After initially falling from a peak in the early 1990s, the number of households in temporary accommodations has risen significantly again since 1997

Households ('000)

Source: ODPM quarterly statistical releases

1.22 In January 2004, the Homelessness Directorate merged with ODPM's Housing Care and Support Division, to form the Homelessness and Housing Support Directorate ("the Directorate") located alongside the Neighbourhood Renewal Unit and the Social Exclusion Unit in ODPM's Tackling Disadvantage Group. Its mission is to tackle homelessness more effectively and help vulnerable people sustain independent living.

1.23 The new Directorate comprises 60 staff, with around half working on homelessness and half on the "Supporting People" programme. Its role is to:

■ promote homelessness prevention and effective implementation of the Homelessness Act 2002;

■ reduce the inappropriate use of Bed & Breakfast accommodation for homeless families with children;

■ reduce the numbers of people sleeping rough;

■ develop approaches to tackling homelessness which result from constructive working across departments;

■ deliver a programme providing housing related support for vulnerable groups, known as "Supporting People"; and

■ improve information and intelligence about the problems and solutions associated with these aims.

The cost of the Directorate's programmes

1.24 In 2004-05, the Directorate allocated just under £60 million to local authorities and a range of voluntary sector bodies to promote improved practices in the prevention and reduction of homelessness.

Figure 13 on page 35 sets out the areas where this funding was directed.

12 The use of temporary accommodation tends to be concentrated in those parts of the country with greater general housing supply pressures

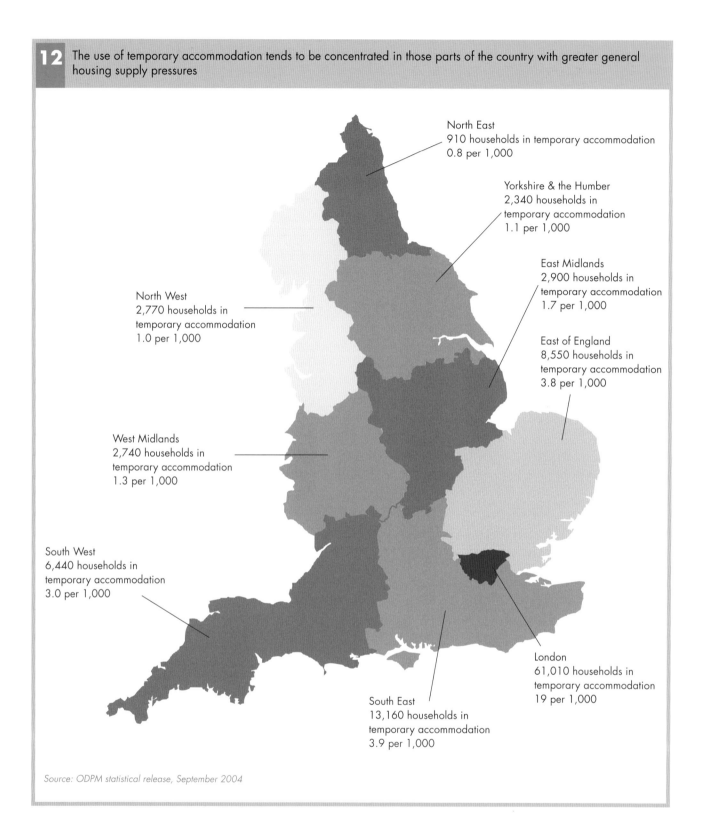

North East
910 households in temporary accommodation
0.8 per 1,000

Yorkshire & the Humber
2,340 households in temporary accommodation
1.1 per 1,000

East Midlands
2,900 households in temporary accommodation
1.7 per 1,000

North West
2,770 households in temporary accommodation
1.0 per 1,000

East of England
8,550 households in temporary accommodation
3.8 per 1,000

West Midlands
2,740 households in temporary accommodation
1.3 per 1,000

South West
6,440 households in temporary accommodation
3.0 per 1,000

London
61,010 households in temporary accommodation
19 per 1,000

South East
13,160 households in temporary accommodation
3.9 per 1,000

Source: ODPM statistical release, September 2004

13 Three quarters of the Directorate's funding goes to local authorities, and almost half of this is allocated to the London boroughs

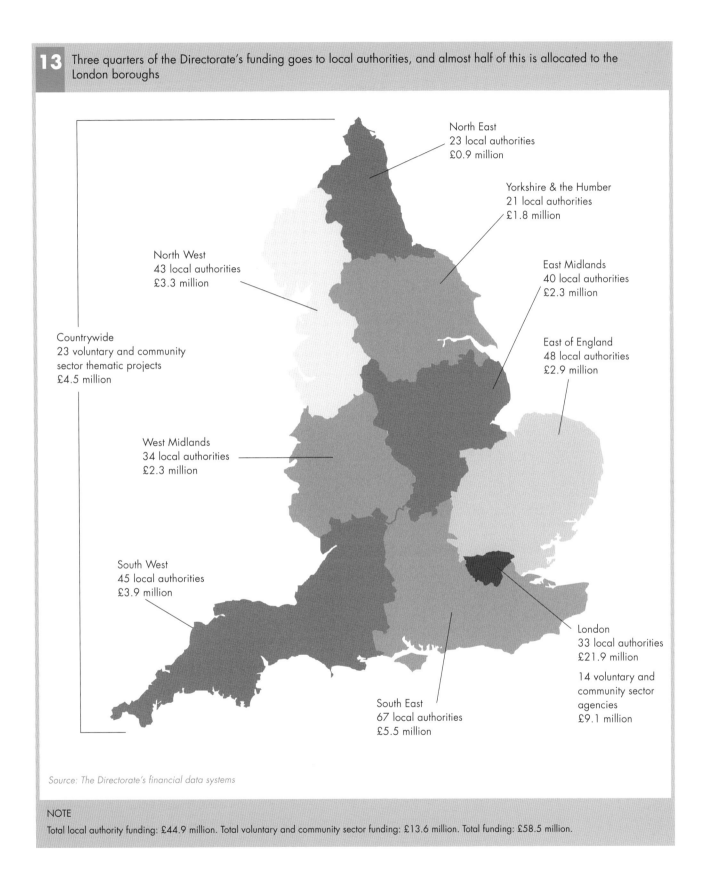

North East
23 local authorities
£0.9 million

Yorkshire & the Humber
21 local authorities
£1.8 million

North West
43 local authorities
£3.3 million

East Midlands
40 local authorities
£2.3 million

Countrywide
23 voluntary and community
sector thematic projects
£4.5 million

East of England
48 local authorities
£2.9 million

West Midlands
34 local authorities
£2.3 million

South West
45 local authorities
£3.9 million

London
33 local authorities
£21.9 million

14 voluntary and
community sector
agencies
£9.1 million

South East
67 local authorities
£5.5 million

Source: The Directorate's financial data systems

NOTE

Total local authority funding: £44.9 million. Total voluntary and community sector funding: £13.6 million. Total funding: £58.5 million.

1.25 The funding for each local authority was made up of a set allocation, based on historical levels of homelessness in that area **(Figure 14)**, and in most cases an additional sum (resulting from a specific bid by the authority) to reward evidence of strong commitment and value for money in the proposed use of resources.

1.26 Additionally, in 2004-05, the Directorate is distributing "Supporting People" funds of over £1.8 billion, of which around £350 million will go to help authorities combat homelessness. This money will enable local authorities to plan, commission and provide support services to those at risk of becoming homeless for the first time, those in temporary accommodation, and those who obtain permanent accommodation having previously been homeless, but may lose it again if they are not given direct financial or other forms of help. Support for other vulnerable groups within the Supporting People programme – such as ex-offenders, substance misusers, and victims of domestic violence – also contributes to the prevention of homelessness.

1.27 Local authorities' Revenue Support Grant has also been increased by £8 million per year in total, to reflect the additional duties placed on them by the Homelessness Act 2002. The Directorate is responsible for an annual resource expenditure (bricks and mortar) budget of £24 million, which is allocated mainly by the Housing Corporation within its Approved Development Programme.

1.28 Funding from the Directorate is normally used to pursue specific local schemes or fund additional staffing posts that are expected to help combat homelessness. Where successful, these resources help to reduce the significant costs to local authorities of providing core homelessness services. The Chartered Institute of Public Finance and Accountancy (CIPFA) calculates that in 2002-03 local authorities spend around £560 million on dealing with homelessness. The cost, net of charges to homeless people and Housing Benefit subsidy, was almost £210 million **(Figure 15)**.

The way the Directorate influences local actions to tackle homelessness

1.29 All local authorities are expected to continue to meet the Government's two key targets, to ensure:

- that, by March 2004, no homeless family with children has to live in a Bed & Breakfast hotel, except in an emergency, and even then for no longer than for six weeks; and

- levels of rough sleeping that are two-thirds below the levels recorded in 1998, or lower.

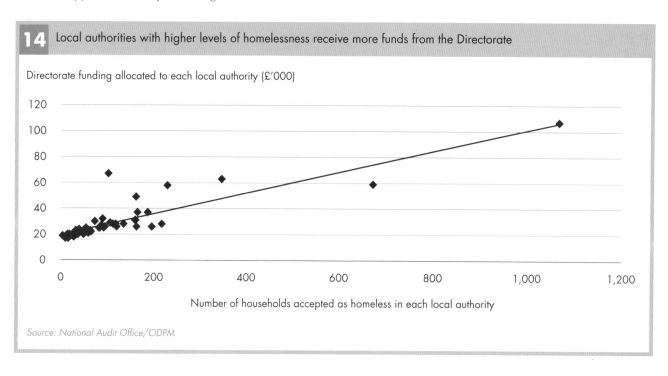

14 Local authorities with higher levels of homelessness receive more funds from the Directorate

Directorate funding allocated to each local authority (£'000)

Number of households accepted as homeless in each local authority

Source: National Audit Office/ODPM

15	The gross cost to local authorities of dealing with homelessness is around £560 million		
Type of expenditure		Gross cost (£m)	Net cost (£m)
Bed & Breakfast accommodation		260	61
Administration and welfare costs		93	93
Leasehold accommodation		78	3
Hostel accommodation		62	9
Other costs		66	43
Total		**559**	**209**

Source: Homelessness Statistics: Actuals 2002-03, CIPFA

1.30 The Directorate has also issued advice on additional positive outcomes that it would like to see local authorities achieve. These outcomes are: reduced levels of repeat homelessness, reduced levels of homelessness against main causes, and reduced inappropriate use of temporary accommodation.

1.31 This does not represent statutory guidance, and the Directorate has not set universal targets against these outcomes, although local authorities are encouraged to set their own local targets. In addition, those authorities receiving over £50,000 in funding are required, as a condition of grant, to set themselves at least one additional outcome, those receiving over £100,000 must set two, and those receiving over £250,000 must set three.

1.32 The Directorate's message is clear: authorities should agree with their local partners, such as voluntary and community groups active in the area, what aims, objectives or targets they should set within their homelessness strategies. However, local authorities' willingness to set local objectives, their performance against the Government's two key targets, and any additional positive outcomes, will influence the Directorate's funding allocations in future years.

We examined progress against the two targets, and evaluated the progress in encouraging more co-ordinated responses to tackling homelessness

1.33 We measured progress against the Directorate's two key targets which focus on some of the most vulnerable groups of homeless people by consulting local authorities, voluntary and community groups and homeless people themselves. We also assessed the work that the Directorate is doing to ensure that homelessness is tackled more effectively at a local and national level. Appendix A describes our work in more detail.

PART TWO

Progress and impact of the Directorate's two key targets

2.1 The Directorate has two key targets, to ensure:

a that, by March 2004, local authorities will ensure that no homeless family with children has to live in a Bed & Breakfast hotel, except in an emergency, and even then for no longer than for six weeks;

b levels of rough sleeping that are two-thirds below the levels recorded in 1998, or lower.

This part of the report examines progress against these two targets.

2.2 The targets are not directly focused on reducing the headline numbers of homeless people. However, the targets are important because they focus on homeless groups who are most likely to experience ill-effects from their housing situation. The Bed & Breakfast target is designed to stop children from living in poor quality accommodation, where their social, health and educational development is likely to be badly compromised. The rough sleeping target focuses on the most visible form of homelessness. It aims to encourage those who are severely marginalised, and who often have complex needs, back towards mainstream society.

2.3 Our main findings for the Bed & Breakfast target were:

■ Many units of Bed & Breakfast accommodation are of poor quality, supporting the need for this target.

■ Meeting the target and moving large numbers of families out of Bed & Breakfast accommodation was a significant achievement.

■ Between March 2004 (the target date) and September 2004, there was a slight increase in the number of families with children in Bed & Breakfast accommodation for more than six weeks. There will probably continue to be a small number of exceptional cases who stay for more than six weeks, and these numbers need to be monitored closely.

■ Rapid progress was achieved through proactive and targeted efforts by the Directorate.

■ Moving people out of Bed & Breakfast accommodation has delivered cost savings for local authorities, which may amount to £40-50 million each year.

■ Alternatives to Bed & Breakfast accommodation are generally better, but standards are still variable.

■ The target has produced some wider positive impacts.

2.4 Our main findings for the rough sleeping target were:

■ The number of rough sleepers has declined beyond the target level, at a time when wider homelessness pressures were increasing.

■ Partnership working is crucial in providing effective services to rough sleepers.

■ More evidence is needed about the route from hostel to "move-on" accommodation.

a) The Bed & Breakfast target

Many units of Bed & Breakfast accommodation are of poor quality

2.5 Our qualitative research demonstrated the poor conditions in some Bed & Breakfast accommodation. The homeless families we talked to often referred to the cramped conditions, the lack of cooking facilities, and the perceived lack of safety (**Case Example 1**). This evidence strongly supports the need for the target to be set, met and sustained.

Meeting the target and moving large numbers of families out of Bed & Breakfast accommodation was a significant achievement

2.6 The Bed & Breakfast target was announced in March 2002. At this point, 6,700 families with dependent children were living in Bed & Breakfast accommodation. At the target date of 31 March 2004, there were only 28 families who had been in Bed & Breakfast accommodation for more than six weeks. **Figure 16** shows how progress was made towards the target. We estimate that up to 24,000 families had a shorter stay in Bed & Breakfast accommodation as a result of the target (**Figure 17**).

2.7 The Homelessness (Suitability of Accommodation) (England) Order 2003, which came into force on 1 April 2004, enshrined the Bed & Breakfast target in the homelessness legislation. The Order gives families the power to take local authorities to court if they are placed in Bed & Breakfast accommodation for more than the six week limit.

16	Between March 2002 and March 2004 there was a dramatic fall in the number of families with children in Bed & Breakfast accommodation but the number has risen slightly since March 2004

Date	Number of families with children in Bed & Breakfast accommodation	Number in Bed & Breakfast accommodation for over 6 weeks
March 2002	6,700	4,000 (estimated)
June 2002	6,700	4,000 (estimated)
September 2002	6,700	4,000 (estimated)
December 2002	5,600	3,600
March 2003	4,800	2,810
June 2003	3,730	1,980
September 2003	3,190	1,600
December 2003	1,680	930
March 2004	830	28
June 2004	1,050	60
September 2004	1,370	167

Source: ODPM quarterly statistical releases

17	We estimate that around 24,000 households have benefited from the Bed & Breakfast target

There are no hard data on how many households have avoided Bed & Breakfast accommodation or had their stays in such accommodation reduced as a result of the target, not least because this involves counting events which did not happen. However, it is possible to make an estimate:

- We took the number of families in Bed & Breakfast accommodation for six weeks or more (at the first point that this information is available, December 2002), as a proportion of new households being accepted as homeless in the quarter October-December 2002.

- From this we calculated how many families we might have expected to be in long-term Bed & Breakfast accommodation at the end of following quarters.

- By taking the difference between the expected and actual numbers recorded between March 2003 and December 2004, we estimated that 24,000 families avoided a long stay in Bed & Breakfast accommodation.

This estimate has some limitations - for example, it does not count the families assisted between March and December 2002 or the families helped through new prevention activities to avoid homelessness altogether. But there is also an element of double counting as some families remained in Bed & Breakfast for more than three months. However, the estimate provides an indication of the magnitude of local authorities' achievements.

CASE EXAMPLE 1

The poor quality of much Bed & Breakfast accommodation

"Me and my partner were in the smallest room possible... I had holes in the bathroom floor where you could see the pipe work... When I went into hospital with my son I said 'You'll have to ring the Council, I can't bring a newborn baby into that room'... And it was only because my health visitor got in touch with the Council that we actually got pushed forward into the hostel."

Ex-Bed & Breakfast, West Wiltshire (quote from focus group)

"I was only there for three weeks, so I could not really say I stayed there for too long, but from what I've seen there... it's terrible, I mean everybody's got problems, but I think certain places should be more secure. You know, try and crack down on drugs because I know sometimes you see either alcoholics or drunkards... as a pregnant woman I was a bit afraid...the room was alright though, there was not a toilet inside, but a shower and a sink and you could cook in there, but the toilet was missing, it was quite awkward, there was like a shared toilet outside."

Ex-Bed & Breakfast, Lambeth (quote from interview)

"Me and my partner have been split up – he's upstairs and I'm downstairs you know... you have to share as well with people... even if you're not a drug addict, the landlady would put you into a room with someone who is..."

Rough sleeper who was in Bed & Breakfast accommodation, Doncaster (quote from interview)

Source: National Audit Office qualitative research

2.8 The Directorate challenged each of the 17 local authorities responsible for the remaining 28 families at the end of March 2004. In each case, there was an operational or case-related reason why the target was not met. All of the families were moved by early May 2004.

Between March and September 2004, the number of families in Bed & Breakfast accommodation for six weeks rose slightly

2.9 While the reduction in use of Bed & Breakfast accommodation has been achieved mainly through a greater emphasis on preventing homelessness, it is likely that wider housing market trends have also been favourable to local authorities in meeting the target. For example, the popularity of buy-to-let has increased the stock of privately rented properties, and average rents have fallen in many parts of the country. The local authorities that we visited told us that a fall in supply in the private rental market could seriously affect their ability to place families quickly into alternatives to Bed & Breakfast accommodation.

2.10 The new legislation, which gives the target a statutory basis, allows some exemptions, for example where authorities are exercising discretionary power to accommodate a family. It is therefore likely that a small number of families will remain in Bed & Breakfast accommodation for more than six weeks. As Figure 16 shows, the use of Bed & Breakfast hotels increased slightly after the target date of March 2004 – in part due to the exemptions allowed – although the number of families resident for more than six weeks remained 96 per cent lower than at March 2002 when the target was set. The Directorate informed us that the number was likely to have fallen again by December 2004, although official data for this period will not be available until March 2005.

2.11 We were told of a few cases where, in pursuit of the target, local authorities moved households out of Bed & Breakfast accommodation when they were only a few weeks away from acquiring permanent accommodation, or where a period of physical upheaval, often following on closely from a previous move, presented difficulties for the family. However, very many authorities, including a large number with severe homelessness and housing pressures, were able to avoid these difficulties.

2.12 In one case, where action had not been taken in time to avoid a family remaining for more than six weeks, the local authority decided to resist the strictures of the target where it felt this was in the best interests of the homeless family (**Case Example 2**).

Rapid progress was achieved through proactive and targeted efforts by the Directorate

2.13 Around three-quarters of the local authorities responding to our survey agreed or strongly agreed that this target was the right priority to address. More importantly, many staff in our case study areas stressed that they had serious doubts about whether the target was achievable, and that the help which the Directorate provided was a crucial factor in convincing them that sufficient alternatives to Bed & Breakfast accommodation could be found. The Directorate also worked with the Department for Work and Pensions to review housing benefit procedures and provide extra incentives for local authorities to place families in alternatives to Bed & Breakfast accommodation.

CASE EXAMPLE 2

Meeting the target versus meeting the needs of the family

Harrogate Borough Council failed to meet the Bed & Breakfast target because one family had remained in this type of temporary accommodation for longer than six weeks beyond the target deadline.

The R family were a couple with a newly born child. The father worked night shifts in a local supermarket. The nearest alternative accommodation available at the time of the target deadline was 13 miles away, and as the family did not own a car, relocation would have seriously affected his ability to travel to work.

The R family decided to remain in their Bed & Breakfast accommodation in their home town until more suitable housing became available. The total length of stay was seven weeks.

The Council was reminded that the target has a statutory basis and failure to comply would place them at risk of legal challenge, judicial review, close monitoring or reduced grant funding.

Source: ODPM

2.14 The Directorate used special advisors and carefully targeted funding to achieve the Bed & Breakfast target. Just under £25 million was allocated to local authorities who faced the biggest challenges in moving families out of Bed & Breakfast accommodation. The most common types of action that local authorities took in pursuit of the target are set out at **Figure 18**.

2.15 Funding from the Directorate encouraged many local authorities to adopt innovative approaches that they would otherwise have not developed. **Case Example 3** sets out a new approach adopted by the London Borough of Lambeth.

Moving people out of Bed & Breakfast accommodation has delivered cost savings

2.16 Bed & Breakfast accommodation is an expensive option, since local authorities are effectively paying hotel rates on a per night basis. By comparison, private sector leasing schemes or one-off rental agreements with landlords are often considerably cheaper. **Figure 19** sets out the comparative costs for a sample of local authorities.

CASE EXAMPLE 3

"Lettings First"

Lettings First is a partnership arrangement set up by Lambeth Council to develop sustainable alternatives to housing families in Bed & Breakfast accommodation. It was funded by a grant from the Directorate.

The scheme involved setting up an agency that resembled a traditional estate agency, to shift public perception of working with a local authority and eliminate the stigma associated with being homeless. It aimed to encourage better working relationships with landlords in the borough and encourage more of them to allow their properties to be used for homeless people and those on low incomes.

Between November 2002 and July 2003, 235 families were transferred out of Bed & Breakfast accommodation. A further 77 families were moved into self-contained accommodation in the private sector supported by a rent deposit scheme promoted by Lettings First.

The scheme helped Lambeth to meet the Bed & Breakfast target eight months before the 31 March 2004 deadline.

Source: Lambeth Council

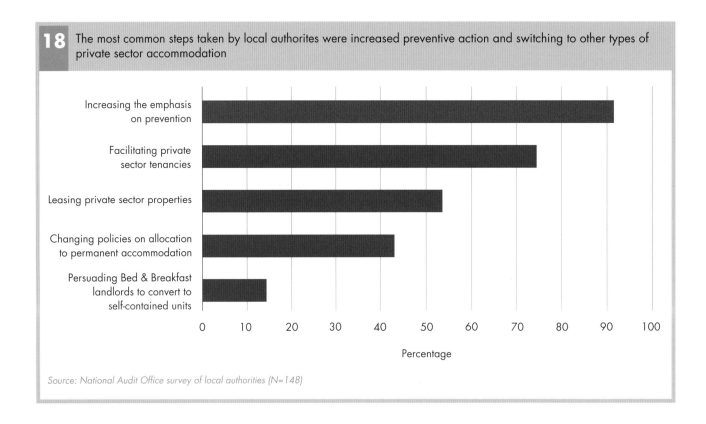

18 The most common steps taken by local authorites were increased preventive action and switching to other types of private sector accommodation

Percentage

Source: National Audit Office survey of local authorities (N=148)

19	Local authorities have secured significant cost savings by switching to alternative types of temporary accommodation		

Local Authority	Cost of housing a family of four in Bed & Breakfast accommodation (per week)	Cost of housing a family of four in alternative accommodation (per week)
Lambeth	£600	£220
Brent	£430	£350
Manchester	£355	£250
Croydon	£300	£210

Source: Local authorities' Housing and Homelessness Departments

2.17 There is currently no aggregated information on the savings that local authorities have achieved by moving away from Bed & Breakfast accommodation. This would be difficult to identify separately because of changes in the flow of homelessness cases. However, given that the prevailing use of this accommodation has fallen by around 6,000 families per year (Figure 16), if similar savings to those shown in Figure 18 were achieved in other local authorities, then total savings could be around £40-50 million.

2.18 Our case study authorities felt strongly that the targeted funding available from the Directorate was a crucial factor in allowing them to address the target. Such funding has encouraged authorities to try out new approaches and to "mainstream" them where successful **(Case Example 4)**.

2.19 A number of local authorities explained that they faced increased administrative problems because of the nature of the accommodation they now provided. For example, where they have procured a large number of units through a private sector leasing scheme, the units are likely to be located across a wide geographical area. This makes it difficult for them to manage the properties well and to respond promptly where problem arise, although they recognise that financial savings for them and improved conditions for those being housed outweigh these administrative difficulties.

CASE EXAMPLE 4

Cost savings at West Wiltshire District Council

In 2003-04, West Wiltshire District Council spent £656,000 on Bed & Breakfast accommodation for homeless households. The figure was expected to reach £1,000,000 in 2004-05. The Directorate awarded the Council a Bed & Breakfast reduction grant of £50,000 to help them find ways to move families out of such accommodation.

The Council has reduced expenditure to an estimated £56,000 for 2004-05. They achieved this by investing the grant in prevention schemes and alternative approaches such as securing accessing private leased homes for temporary accommodation.

Source: West Wiltshire District Council

Alternatives to Bed & Breakfast accommodation are generally better, but standards are still variable

2.20 The primary aim of moving families with children out of Bed & Breakfast accommodation was to improve their general surroundings and quality of life. Over 80 per cent of local authorities responding to our survey agreed that the quality of temporary accommodation that they now use is better than that used previously.

2.21 In our qualitative research, we interviewed 18 individuals who had been in Bed & Breakfast accommodation but were moved into other types of accommodation. Almost all believed that their situation had improved. Typical reactions are shown in **Case Example 5**.

2.22 Existing statutory standards apply to all temporary accommodation used, and there is guidance on how to ensure that accommodation is suitable for the households placed in it. However, no information is collected centrally on the quality of accommodation used. The Greater London Authority's Housing and Homelessness Unit told us that not all London boroughs carry out inspections or take enforcement action as regularly as they should.

2.23 The Directorate is working on a revised "Homelessness Code of Guidance" which is intended to:

- set out more clearly the minimum standards that should apply to all forms of temporary accommodation;

- set out additional standards for Bed & Breakfast hotels used as temporary accommodation; and

- provide guidance on arrangements to ensure that homeless households placed in temporary accommodation receive support to ensure that their health, education and welfare needs are met.

2.24 During our study we visited 25 units of temporary accommodation in four case study areas. While these properties are not representative of all accommodation used across the country, they illustrate the wide range of quality, covering some very good accommodation and some less good, including:

- newly refurbished two-bedroom flats above shops acquired through private sector leasing;

CASE EXAMPLE 5

Moving out of Bed & Breakfast accommodation

"It's much better... I mean it's much better than the Bed & Breakfast, definitely... I know a lot of people who will say you've done well because of this space, for one person and a baby, you know, this kitchen is really nice..."

Ex-Bed & Breakfast, Lambeth (quote from interview)

"I've got two bedrooms, a nice living room... a toilet, a bathroom... it's not my ideal home, but it's nice."

Ex-Bed & Breakfast, Doncaster (quote from group discussion)

Source: National Audit Office qualitative research

- one bedroom flats being used as 'self-contained hostels' for families of four;

- old-style Bed & Breakfast rooms, which were being refurbished and amalgamated to provide much better quality self-contained apartments;

- family hostels in converted houses on busy roads, with very little outside play area for children, and shared facilities. In one, cooking facilities, three beds and living space were contained in a single room; and

- three-bedroom flats in a run-down Victorian mansion block with a defective front door, low light levels in some rooms and tiny kitchens.

The Bed & Breakfast target for families has produced some wider positive impacts

2.25 In many cases, the approaches used to move families out of Bed & Breakfast accommodation have been used for other homeless groups. Staff in the case study local authorities that we visited were generally agreed that they had a responsibility to reduce the use of Bed & Breakfast accommodation for all client groups. Around 45 per cent of local authorities responding to our survey believed that services to other homeless people had improved as a result of the Bed & Breakfast target, and a similar proportion had begun to move other groups of homeless people out of this type of accommodation.

b) The rough sleeping target

Rough sleepers are a visible and often excluded group

2.26 The rough sleeping target was established to address the most visible form of homelessness. Rough sleepers often have multiple difficulties – drug and alcohol dependencies, mental health problems, a history of prison sentences or spells in care. Getting rough sleepers off the streets is therefore not simply a matter of offering accommodation, but of providing a package of support.

2.27 Where the Bed & Breakfast target concerns families with children, the rough sleeping target focuses mainly on single people. While virtually all families with children will be in priority need of accommodation under the homelessness legislation, it is a matter of individual circumstances as to whether any particular single person falls into the "priority need" category and therefore has a statutory right to be housed. Indeed many rough sleepers, because of their personal circumstances, may not make a homelessness application in the first place.

2.28 Perhaps because of this lack of certainty over priority need, or more likely because rough sleeping is an issue only in certain localities, only just over half of the local authorities responding to our survey agreed or strongly agreed that the rough sleeping target was the right priority to address. By contrast, the figure among voluntary and community sector groups, who play a more active role in providing support to rough sleepers and other single homeless people, was over two-thirds.

The recorded number of rough sleepers has declined beyond the target level

2.29 Official data on rough sleepers are compiled by asking those local authorities who consider that they have a rough sleeping problem to carry out a street count. Where no recent count has taken place, authorities are asked to estimate the number sleeping rough on a single night. These counts and estimates show that the number of rough sleepers has declined by over 70 per cent since 1998 **(Figure 20)**. Given the nature of rough sleeping and the problems that people who are sleeping rough face, and the wider homelessness pressures that have existed in recent years, meeting and sustaining this target has been a significant achievement.

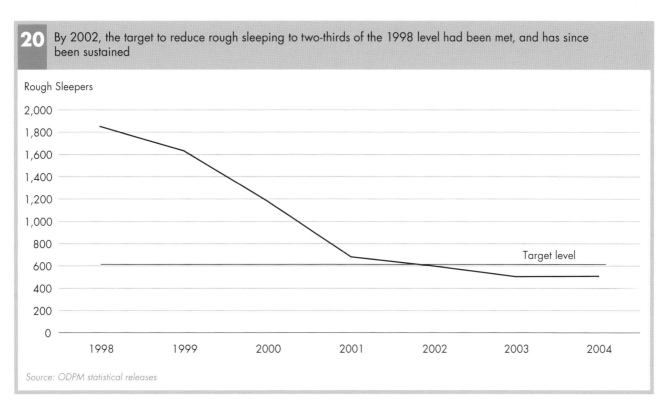

20 By 2002, the target to reduce rough sleeping to two-thirds of the 1998 level had been met, and has since been sustained

Rough Sleepers

Target level

1998　1999　2000　2001　2002　2003　2004

Source: ODPM statistical releases

2.30 Although the 70 per cent reduction in rough sleeping at a national level has been a significant achievement, there has been considerable variation in performance between regions **(Figure 21)**. Not every region has achieved or sustained a two-thirds reduction. In London, numbers have fallen, but not by two-thirds compared with 1998. Westminster alone currently has two-thirds of the 265 rough sleepers in the capital, and has reduced numbers to 73 per cent of the 1998 level. The remaining London Boroughs had met the target by 2004. The numbers of rough sleepers in the East Midlands and the North West have declined below target levels but have risen slightly in 2004 so that they just exceed two-thirds below the 1998 level (by two and four people, respectively).

2.31 The Directorate gathers information on the number of rough sleepers as at June each year. The information shows the results of recent street counts for every area in which a count has taken place. Where no count has taken place, local authorities must submit an estimate, although any estimate that shows more than ten rough sleepers must be validated by a count. For all other areas, zero estimates are assumed on the basis of local authorities' statistical returns.

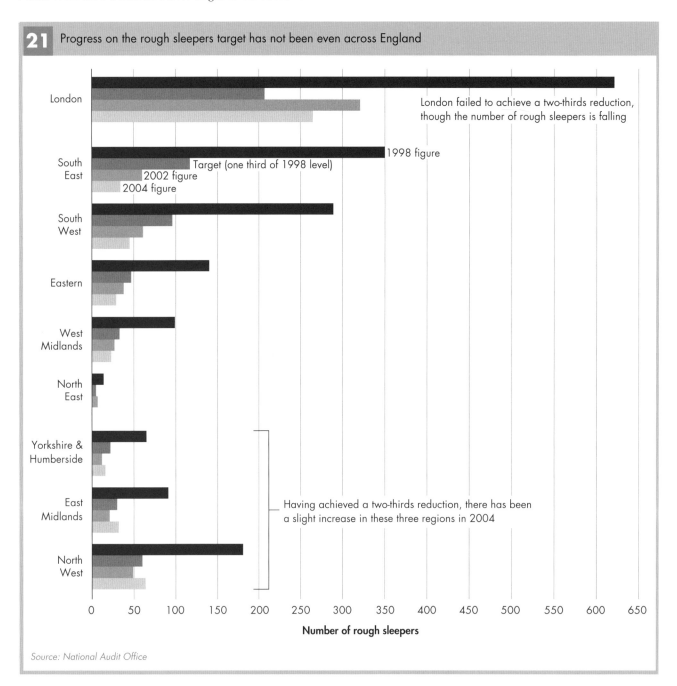

21 Progress on the rough sleepers target has not been even across England

Source: National Audit Office

2.32 The count is designed to capture the number of people sleeping rough on a given night rather than over the course of a year. Counts might not capture all of those sleeping rough, but because the methodology has been applied consistently area-to-area and year-on-year, it is the most accurate measure of the relative scale of the problem and change over time.

2.33 Much rough sleeping is intermittent. Local authorities and voluntary agencies deal with much larger numbers throughout the course of the year. The Directorate has collected information and commissioned research which suggests that the number of people sleeping rough over the course of a year may be ten times the number on a single night.[13] Some 38 of the local authorities responding to our survey had helped to resettle rough sleepers during 2003-04. Between them, they assisted around 3,500 rough sleepers by getting them access to hostels, Bed & Breakfast accommodation, other forms of temporary accommodation and permanent tenancies.

Partnership working is crucial in providing effective services to rough sleepers

2.34 Given the nature of this client group, local authorities adopted a range of new measures to address the target. Over three-quarters of local authorities responding to our survey made greater use of voluntary and community sector partners, and two-thirds developed their links with health and addiction services **(Case Example 6)**. The types of new activity carried out in pursuit of the target included:

- widening the range of accommodation, including specialist and move-on units;

- extending the use of night shelters;

- employing more outreach workers; and

- expanding their work on welfare and mental health issues.

2.35 We asked local authorities a number of questions about the benefits of having the target in place. Their responses are set out in **Figure 22 (overleaf)**.

2.36 Our qualitative research and case study visits uncovered many examples of successful partnership working. Typical approaches are set out in **Case Example 7 and Case Example 8.**

CASE EXAMPLE 6

The impact of outreach workers

"I got in with some outreach workers that would come round and they would visit you on the street... they got me on the list for sheltered accommodation and they had me on the list for some months and then eventually a place came up in King George's hostel... I was there for seven or eight months and during that time they had key workers at the hostel that helped me because I was on drugs and all that. They helped me with the drug issues and once I was stable I was put onto a housing list and when that became available and I was ready, I moved into this flat."

Ex-rough sleeper, Lambeth (quote from interview)

Source: National Audit Office qualitative research

CASE EXAMPLE 7

Partnership working in Doncaster

In Doncaster, many of those we interviewed had been helped after contacting a night shelter. Once they got a bed there, if they were drug-free or on a programme to become drug-free they could be offered accommodation in the 24-hour supported hostel run by the M25 charity or other supported accommodation.

"When you go to Union Street [the night shelter] that's where it all begins. They refer you to see a worker, they'll make an action plan to find out what help you need..."

Ex-rough sleeper, Doncaster (quote from interview)

Source: National Audit Office qualitative research

CASE EXAMPLE 8

Partnership working in Manchester

The City Centre Project is a not-for-profit organisation working with 16-25 year olds. It has two teams:

- Homelessness Prevention Services, running a café for drop-in advice every morning. They offer a free breakfast, showers, laundry and contact with youth workers who work with other agencies on drug, sexual health and mental health matters. Some clients are rough sleepers who need help out of short-term difficulties. They have no accommodation, but refer clients to a direct access hostel.

- Housing Support Services, which organises 50 housing units funded by Supporting People funding. A Registered Social Landlord owns the housing, while the City Centre Project provides the support. Around 80 clients move through the accommodation every year, and the support programme can last for up to two years.

Source: National Audit Office

---

13   Randall G & Brown S, (2002), Helping Rough Sleepers Off The Street, ODPM.

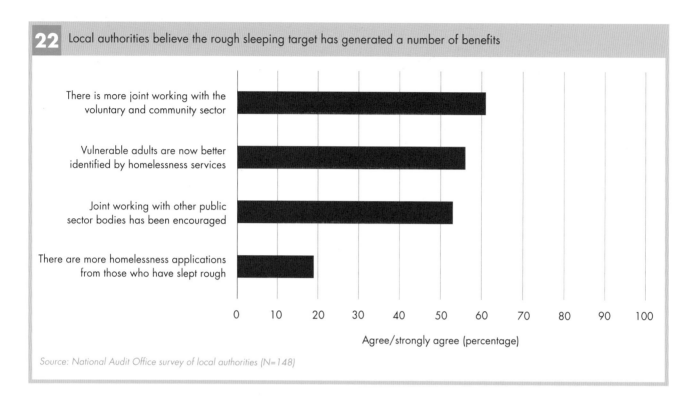

22 Local authorities believe the rough sleeping target has generated a number of benefits

There is more joint working with the
voluntary and community sector

Vulnerable adults are now better
identified by homelessness services

Joint working with other public
sector bodies has been encouraged

There are more homelessness applications
from those who have slept rough

0   10   20   30   40   50   60   70   80   90   100

Agree/strongly agree (percentage)

Source: National Audit Office survey of local authorities (N=148)

More evidence is needed about the route from hostel to "move-on" accommodation

2.37 Since rough sleepers often have complex problems, they are particularly likely to fall into a pattern of repeat homelessness. They therefore need help to address their most pressing initial problems, and then access different types of accommodation (often referred to as "move-on" accommodation) to help their rehabilitation back into normal life.

2.38 Westminster Council, which has by far the highest rough sleeper count in the country, carried out a review of hostels in mid-2004. Of the 700 people who moved on from rough sleeping hostels in 2003-04, half did so in a structured way. The other half left as an abandonment or eviction, or by their own arrangements. Many abandonments were part of a long-standing pattern of such behaviour and occurred only after efforts by hostel staff to avoid it. The average length of stay in rough sleeping hostels was almost nine months, although there was considerable variation even among people looking for similar types of accommodation. The review noted that most of the rough sleepers' hostels were large, general purpose facilities, with

less than one in ten beds being in any sense specialist. It concluded that the wait for structured move-on was not excessive, but that the extent of unstructured move-on showed that there were significant numbers of people who did not engage with, or necessarily need, the full resettlement service set up in most hostels.

2.39 A survey on hostels carried out by the Greater London Authority in 2003 concluded that around 30 per cent of residents were ready to move on but there was no suitable accommodation for them. There was a particular need for independent (no or low support) move-on accommodation. This suggests that many people are waiting to move on, not because they have complex support needs at that time, but because there is simply an insufficient supply of general housing units.

PART THREE
Progress in developing new approaches to tackling homelessness

3.1 In Part 2 we examined the impact of the Government's two key targets which aim to improve the experience of families and individuals who have already found themselves homeless. This part of the report examines the progress that has been made in developing more responsive approaches that focus on preventing families or individuals becoming homeless in the first place. It examines:

a the impact of the Directorate in developing more co-ordinated policy across Whitehall;

b local progress, including the impact of the statutory requirement on local authorities to develop a homelessness strategy.[14]

3.2 We found that, in relation to developing more co-ordinated policy across Whitehall, the Directorate:

■ has given a new focus to tacking homelessness across government;

■ has worked with a number of Departments to develop new approaches to preventing homelessness amongst particular groups;

■ is helping to influence the provision of services to drug and alcohol misusers but faces challenges in ensuring the health needs of the homeless are addressed;

■ is taking action to help ensure the Supporting People programme delivers value for money;

■ needs to work with the National Asylum Support Service to develop more co-ordinated approaches;

■ needs to work closely with the Housing Corporation to ensure Registered Social Landlords help local authorities meet the needs of homeless people.

3.3 In relation to local progress and strategy making:

■ strategies have helped to raise the profile of homelessness issues and the need to tackle them;

■ strategies have led to stronger partnerships in many areas;

■ strategies have led to changes in approach;

■ the Directorate has identified a number of areas for further improvement in the strategies;

■ more needs to be done to identify and spread good practice on what works cost-effectively; and

■ the Directorate should consider clarifying the role of Government Offices in tackling homelessness.

14   We draw upon the independent evaluation of Local Authority strategies commissioned by ODPM and carried out concurrently with our study.

a) The impact of the Directorate

The establishment of the Directorate has given a new focus to tackling homelessness within Whitehall

3.4 The Government's 2002 policy paper "More Than A Roof" recognised that a more co-ordinated approach from central Government was required to tackle homelessness as a symptom of social exclusion rather than just a lack of a roof. A wide range of Departments, agencies and Non-Departmental Public Bodies have a potential role in helping to develop new responses to homelessness and to help in identifying and implementing new ways of preventing it **(Figure 23)**.

3.5 The bringing together of the former Rough Sleepers Unit, the Bed & Breakfast Unit and a new homelessness team within the Directorate has provided a clearer focus for policy development and coordination on homelessness issues. The Directorate funds programmes to positively influence the way that homelessness is tackled at a local level, provides specialist advice and guidance, collates data and evaluates more qualitative information in support of good practice. In addition, it pilots new initiatives and is responsible for co-ordinating partnership working with other central government departments and agencies **(Figure 24)**.

---

23 The Directorate has secured funds from other sources to benefit homeless people

Partners	Amount/period	Purpose
Department of Health	£1,900,000 2002-03	To Westminster City Council, for rough sleepers with mental health problems and potential rough sleepers
Department of Health	£1m (probable) 2005-06	To the Gordon Hospital, London to support people vulnerable to rough sleeping due to mental health problems
National Institute for Mental Health in England	£39,000 2004-05	For joint research and guidance on services to homeless people with challenging behaviour/dual diagnoses, and those in temporary accommodation with mental health issues
Home Office	£1,000,000	Contributing to a package of support for ukrefugesonline, a domestic violence helpline and additional refuge spaces
Home Office Confiscated Assets Fund	£1,000,000 2001-02	For drug treatment in areas outside of London with the highest number of drug-misusing rough sleepers
Department for Work and Pensions	£10,000,000 over 2002-03	To encourage local authorities to use alternative forms of temporary accommodation rather than Bed & Breakfast
London Boroughs, Association of London Government, GLA, London Connects	£260,000	To develop and implement 'NOTIFY', a computer system which will help local authorities work in partnership with key organisations locally to target support services for households in temporary accommodation, especially those moving between different housing authorities
National Learning and Skills Council	£400,000 2004 to 2006	Skills training and accreditation for homelessness workers and self-development/esteem building programmes for homeless people

Source: National Audit Office

24 The Directorate works creatively to influence policy development and services

It funds programmes:

- Allocating over £1 million for 22 extra bed spaces at the Sir Oswald Stoll Mansions hostel for vulnerable ex-service personnel with mental and/or physical disabilities.

It advises, guides and supports:

- Exploring the Department for Work and Pensions' proposals in *Building on the New Deal* to improve access and support to work and benefits for homeless people.

- Working with the JobCentre Plus London Homeless Services Team to tailor benefit claim procedures to the needs of vulnerable homeless people.

It evaluates good practice:

- With Brighton and Hove City Council, testing ways to protect people vulnerable to homelessness from the impact of direct payment of housing benefit and flat-rate housing benefit pathfinders.

It pilots initiatives:

- Establishing the number and location of rough sleeping ex-forces personnel, as part of a joint programme of work with the Ministry of Defence.

- Approaching the Football Foundation and Department of Culture, Media and Sport for funding and support to establish a five-a-side football Street League to build homeless people's fitness and self-esteem.

It influences other government departments and agencies:

- Ensuring that the Department of Health's indicators for tackling health inequalities includes specific indicators for homeless families.

Source: National Audit Office

The Directorate has worked with a number of Departments to develop new approaches to preventing homelessness amongst particular groups

Prisoners

3.6 Offenders and ex-offenders have particular difficulties in obtaining accommodation, yet homelessness is related to recidivism.[15] In 2002, following consultation with commentators and voluntary and community organisations, the Directorate secured changes to legislation to make ex-prisoners who are vulnerable a priority need group for whom local authorities have a statutory duty to secure housing.

3.7 The Directorate chairs an accommodation sub-board as part of the Reducing Re-offending National Action Plan. This seeks to address the accommodation needs of offenders by building systems:

- to assess prisoners' housing needs better;

- to collect and share information about prisoners' housing needs; and

- to test new approaches to housing advice and prevention of homelessness.

3.8 The Directorate has piloted housing advice centres through voluntary agencies working in a number of prisons and Young Offender Institutions. These address the housing needs of women prisoners, those with mental health and/or substance abuse problems, those from inner city prisons and young offenders. In 2002, responsibility for these projects was transferred to the Home Office.

Victims of domestic violence

3.9 Domestic violence is a major cause of homelessness. The Directorate's priorities are to help develop a range of routes to help and advise those suffering domestic violence and to foster a range of suppliers of hostel accommodation, widening the supply of refuge accommodation. More recently, the Directorate has begun to advance the prevention agenda with the Home Office by encouraging joint development of schemes which allow the victims of domestic violence to stay in their original homes (**Case Example 9**).

CASE EXAMPLE 9

Barnet Sanctuary Project

The Barnet 'Sanctuary Project' is a victim-centred initiative which provides additional security measures to the homes of domestic violence survivors. The scheme aims to make it possible for victims to remain in their homes and feel safe, enabling families to avoid homelessness and the upheaval of moving. Typically, the project installs new and extra locks and lighting, and creates a 'safe room' with lockable, solid-core door, grilles on the window and a link to the police within the home.

Since December 2003, the project has installed 36 sanctuaries. At an annual estimated cost of £55,000 the spend is a fraction of the estimated £600,000 in temporary accommodation costs for 36 families for a year. It is funded half by the Barnet Safer Communities Project (Home Office) and half by the London Borough of Barnet. Since the start of the scheme Barnet has seen fewer cases of homelessness due to domestic violence, and the families involved have been very positive.

Source: London Borough of Barnet

---

15   *Prevention is better than cure: New solutions to street homelessness from Crisis,* Randall G and Brown S (1999) Crisis.

Ex-service personnel

3.10 Some ex-service personnel may find it difficult to adapt to civilian life. Early research showed that around 25 per cent of rough sleepers were ex-service personnel.[16] Consequently, the Directorate made vulnerable ex-service personnel a priority need group in 2002. This imposes a duty on local authorities to organise permanent housing for unintentionally homeless, vulnerable ex-service personnel. The Directorate is monitoring the numbers of ex-service personnel identified as statutorily homeless in the data it receives from local authorities.

3.11 The Directorate has contributed funding to a number of schemes to address the needs of ex-service personnel. These include centres which offer advice, support and transitional housing, and programmes to return ex-service personnel to employment.

Young people

3.12 Young people, especially those leaving care, are prone to homelessness, and the impact of homelessness on the impressionable in this group can be particularly severe, leading to involvement in crime, mental health problems and addiction. As part of the drive to identify better and serve a wider range of vulnerable homeless people, 16 and 17-year olds, and care leavers aged 18 to 20, were added to the priority need groups under the homelessness legislation.

3.13 The Directorate and Department for Education and Skills have jointly invested in pilot schemes to provide emergency refuge accommodation and respite care for young people who have run away from home or who are at risk of being expelled from the family home. The Directorate has identified the importance of well co-ordinated services to this group, who often have a wide range of support needs. It has engaged in several projects to improve cross-departmental working and service delivery to young people who are homeless or at risk of homelessness. It has produced the Careleavers Strategies Handbook with the Department of Health, and the Working Together guidance with the Connexions Service.

3.14 At present the housing benefit payable to a single person under the age of 25 is limited to the equivalent of the rent for a single room in shared accommodation. Local authorities told us this makes it difficult to secure accommodation for homeless people aged under 25.

The Directorate is helping to influence the provision of services to drug and alcohol misusers but faces challenges in ensuring the health needs of the homeless are addressed

3.15 The chaotic lifestyles of alcohol and substance misusers are associated with the risk of homelessness. The Directorate has advised the Home Office on where best to direct £1 million from the Confiscated Assets Fund to tackle drug-related homelessness outside of London. In 2002, along with the Home Office, National Treatment Agency for Substance Misuse (NTA) and Department of Health, the Directorate issued guidance[17] to Drug Action Teams and local authorities about commissioning drug treatment services for homeless people across England.

3.16 The Directorate is working with the NTA to ensure that Drug Action Team treatment plans and homelessness strategies are aligned in key areas as part of the treatment planning process for 2005-06. The Directorate, Home Office and NTA issued a briefing paper in December 2004, providing information and practical examples to meet the housing needs of problematic drug misusers. In addition, Throughcare and Aftercare funding available through the Drug Interventions Programme can now be used to complement existing housing-related support for drug misusing offenders prior to and after release from custody. In line with the local homelessness strategy and DAT Treatment Plan, it can be used in the community to support provision such as rent deposit schemes.

3.17 The Directorate's special advisors have acted as advocates for better co-ordination of service delivery, culminating in the joint ODPM and Department of Health strategy document *Shared Health and Homelessness Outcomes* in 2004. In conjunction with the National Institute for Mental Health in England, the Directorate is commissioning research which will evaluate good practice in mental health services for homeless people in temporary accommodation.

3.18 Despite various pieces of work being taken forward, in general, liaison on health issues could be improved if the Department of Health had a single co-ordinating point on homelessness. Instead the issue is part of the portfolio of several different sections, including the Health Inequalities Unit. In 2001, the National Audit Office noted that the then Rough Sleepers Unit had experienced difficulty in joint working, particularly with local health services.[18] Our research noted a need for better joint working centrally.

---

16   Randall G and Brown S (1994), *Falling Out: A research study of homeless ex-service people, Crisis.*
17   Randall G and DrugScope (2002), *Drug services for homeless people: a good practice handbook, ODPM.*
18   Joining Up to Improve Public Services HC 383 2001-2002, 7 December 2001.

The Directorate is taking action to help ensure the Supporting People programme delivers value for money

3.19 The Supporting People programme began in April 2003, drawing together nine different funding programmes, including Transitional Housing Benefit. The programme funds housing related support services for over one million people including victims of domestic violence, older people and those with mental problems.

3.20 From 2004-05, the Directorate is distributing "Supporting People" funds of over £350 million which are earmarked for combating homelessness. This money will enable councils to plan, commission and provide support services to help vulnerable people live independently in their homes **(Figure 25)**. These efforts apply both to those at risk of becoming homeless for the first time, and to those who obtain permanent accommodation having previously been homeless, but may lose it again if they are not given direct financial or other forms of help.

3.21 At present a large proportion of funding is allocated to pre-existing services for which the strategic need is currently being reassessed by Supporting People administering authorities - county councils, London boroughs, unitary authorities and metropolitan boroughs. In 2003, ODPM commissioned an independent review of the Supporting People Programme. The review found wide variations in unit costs between authorities and recommended efficiency savings could be made but that the pace of change needed to be managed to avoid difficulties for service users and small providers. The Department has therefore asked the Audit Commission to undertake detailed inspections in a series of local authorities with high unit costs, alongside their routine inspections of local authorities.

The Directorate needs to prioritise its work with the National Asylum Support Service to develop more co-ordinated approaches

3.22 The National Asylum Support Service (NASS) is responsible for housing destitute asylum seekers while their requests for asylum are being considered. Since 2000, NASS has dispersed approximately 150,000 asylum seekers into temporary accommodation in locations across Great Britain. Some of this accommodation has been provided by consortia of local authorities, and much has also been procured from the private rental market.

3.23 Once granted Indefinite Leave to Remain, asylum seekers are given 28 days to leave NASS property and find alternative accommodation. Some are unable to find their own accommodation during this time and make a homelessness application with their local authority.

25 The Supporting People programme funds a wide range of services to homeless people

Examples of effective and promising services...	...nominated by
'DISH' – a support project where workers go out to drug users, to help prepare them for independent living in the community. Once they have a tenancy, the support continues to ensure it is sustained	South Oxfordshire District Council
Support for households accommodated in the Council's hostels. Enables assistance with benefits and signposting to other sources of help, for example Sure Start	London Borough of Havering
'Turning Point' for people with severe and enduring mental health problems	Royal Borough of Kensington and Chelsea
A permanent night-shelter – providing counselling, skills training, health and housing advice and resettlement work with former rough sleepers	London Borough of Redbridge
'Rainforest Walk' – a supported housing scheme with Look Ahead Housing Association, for young single people 16-24 years	Bracknell Forest Borough Council
Teenage pregnancy project – providing self contained accommodation for teenage mums with low level support needs	Blackpool Borough Council
Domestic Violence Outreach Services – focuses on prevention of homelessness through support, provision of additional security, removing perpetrator	Manchester City Council

Source: National Audit Office, 2004

3.24 In some areas, former asylum seekers given leave to remain have been a key client group for homelessness services. In Yorkshire and the Humber, the largest dispersal area, former asylum seekers who were homeless because they had to leave NASS accommodation made up some 12 per cent of those to whom the local authority accepted it had a duty to secure accommodation during 2002-03 (although this proportion fell to 6.1 per cent in 2003-04).

3.25 Local authorities find it difficult to estimate demand from asylum seekers granted Indefinite Leave to Remain as NASS has been unable to provide information about cases within their boundaries, partly because of data protection issues.

3.26 NASS has a number of under-utilised properties as a result of the decline in the number of asylum seekers since October 2002. These properties were leased under contracts which do not permit use by non-asylum seekers. NASS has ended some contracts for properties that have become surplus to requirements. While it is not clear whether the remaining under-utilised properties are of the right type or in the right location to relieve homelessness pressures, some authorities, for example Manchester City Council, are attempting to negotiate access to these properties for homeless households, though these plans have yet to bear fruit. NASS and the Directorate are jointly to appoint a secondee to examine the scope for making better use of empty NASS properties where alternative uses are appropriate and cost-effective.

The Directorate needs to work closely with the Housing Corporation to ensure Registered Social Landlords help local authorities meet the needs of homeless people

3.27 Local Housing Authorities have responsibility for securing accommodation for households who are homeless and fall within a priority need group. The proportion of social housing owned directly by local authorities has fallen to less than 70 per cent.[19] Many local authorities have transferred stock to Registered Social Landlords or to Arm's Length Management Organisations

3.28 Registered Social Landlords are required by law to co-operate, insofar as is reasonable, with local authorities in meeting the accommodation needs of homeless people. The Housing Corporation's Regulatory Code clarifies that Registered Social Landlords are expected to give reasonable preference to those in housing need and must work with local authorities to enable them to fulfil their duties to the homeless and people in priority housing need. When asked to do so by the local authority, Registered Social Landlords are required to provide a proportion of their stock to local authority nominations and temporary accommodation to the homeless.

3.29 Local authorities negotiate nomination rights as part of these arrangements, which set out the proportion of housing which will be made available to homeless and other households nominated by the Council. The Directorate has embarked on a programme of work to promote effective co-operation between local authorities and Registered Social Landlords in tackling homelessness. It has recently published a good practice guide, in conjunction with the Housing Corporation, Local Government Association and National Housing Federation.

3.30 Some local authorities told us that a number of Registered Social Landlords are unwilling to take nominated homeless families with a history of rent arrears, anti-social behaviour, or higher support needs. Registered Social Landlords may refuse nominations where they have grounds to believe an applicant would not make a suitable tenant, or where insufficient support has been offered to a vulnerable household. But some authorities felt that Registered Social Landlords resist housing the homeless, on the grounds that, as landlords, they must balance the needs of homeless households, who are often economically inactive and require support, against the broader requirement to build balanced, sustainable communities. Local authorities consider this constrains their ability to place the homeless in permanent accommodation. There is a lack of hard evidence to support claims that Registered Social Landlords are acting for these reasons or failing to meet the statutory and regulatory requirements placed on them.

19   NAO Report "Improving social housing through transfer" March 2003.

The Directorate needs to monitor the impact of evictions for anti-social behaviour

3.31 The Anti-Social Behaviour Act offers a number of routes to tackle anti-social behaviour. These include Anti-Social Behaviour Orders and changing the basis of tenancies to a less secure form in order to lever a change in behaviour. But ultimately eviction can follow, should the anti-social behaviour continue

3.32 The Directorate and the Home Office have begun to pilot local solutions to ensure that people displaying anti-social behaviour have access to the services and support they need to change their behaviour rather than face eviction. The Directorate should continue this work and monitor data on evictions due to anti-social behaviour.

b) Local progress, including the impact of the statutory requirement on local authorities to develop a homelessness strategy

Local authorities were required to draw up homelessness strategies

3.33 The 2002 Homelessness Act required local authorities to review homelessness in their area and produce a strategy to address it by July 2003. The aim was to encourage them to take a more comprehensive approach, promoting prevention over traditional responses and taking an overview of future needs. Strategies were required to cover all homeless people and not just those for whom the authority had a duty to secure accommodation.

3.34 The Directorate provided support to local authorities in a number of ways. It issued statutory and good practice guidance, employed advisors to support many local authorities directly, provided additional financial resources and organised a series of conferences and seminars. The process authorities were expected to follow in drawing up their strategies is shown in **Figure 26 overleaf**.

Strategies have helped to raise the profile of homelessness issues and the need to tackle them

3.35 The statutory requirement to review local services to the homeless and develop a strategy by July 2003 has raised the priority that local authorities and other agencies give to homelessness services. Eighty per cent of local authorities and a similar proportion of voluntary and community sector organisations believe the requirement to produce a strategy has raised the profile of homelessness issues within the local authority and the need to tackle them. The high profile of homelessness strategies meant that homelessness and housing officers were able to raise the awareness of this area of work among senior staff. In the local authorities we visited, the profile of homelessness had been raised, not just among local authority staff, but also more widely among public service agencies and local politicians.

Strategies have led to stronger partnerships in many areas

3.36 A wide range of bodies in the public, voluntary and private sectors have a role in delivering services to the homeless. Whilst local housing authorities were expected to take the lead in developing and publishing strategies, other local organisations were expected to be fully involved. The legislation required the social services authority in two-tier districts to give the housing authority assistance in drawing up the strategy. The Directorate, along with the Department of Health, issued guidance to local authorities on partnership in strategy development.

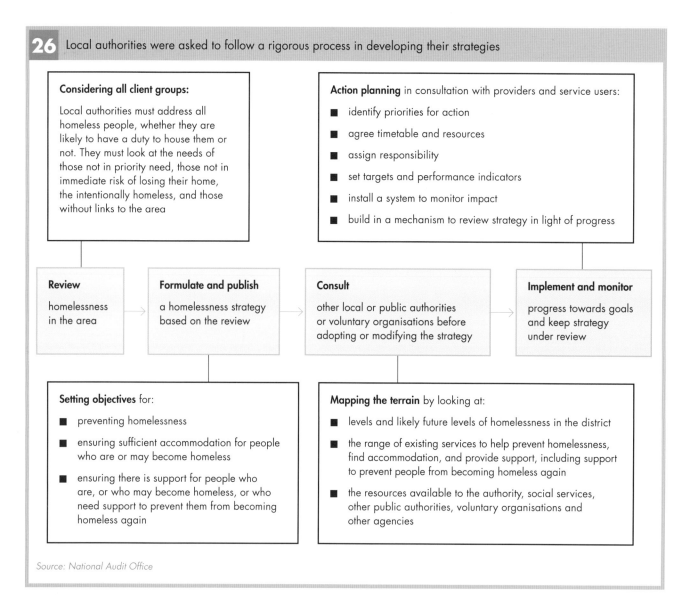

26 Local authorities were asked to follow a rigorous process in developing their strategies

Considering all client groups:

Local authorities must address all homeless people, whether they are likely to have a duty to house them or not. They must look at the needs of those not in priority need, those not in immediate risk of losing their home, the intentionally homeless, and those without links to the area

Action planning in consultation with providers and service users:

■ identify priorities for action

■ agree timetable and resources

■ assign responsibility

■ set targets and performance indicators

■ install a system to monitor impact

■ build in a mechanism to review strategy in light of progress

Review

homelessness in the area

Formulate and publish

a homelessness strategy based on the review

Consult

other local or public authorities or voluntary organisations before adopting or modifying the strategy

Implement and monitor

progress towards goals and keep strategy under review

Setting objectives for:

■ preventing homelessness

■ ensuring sufficient accommodation for people who are or may become homeless

■ ensuring there is support for people who are, or who may become homeless, or who need support to prevent them from becoming homeless again

Mapping the terrain by looking at:

■ levels and likely future levels of homelessness in the district

■ the range of existing services to help prevent homelessness, find accommodation, and provide support, including support to prevent people from becoming homeless again

■ the resources available to the authority, social services, other public authorities, voluntary organisations and other agencies

Source: National Audit Office

3.37 Of all of the benefits which strategy making has delivered, local authorities are most proud of the improvements they have made in multi-agency working and partnership approaches. A large number of local authorities built on or established multi-agency steering groups for guiding the work to carry out reviews and to develop strategies **(Case Example 10)**. **Figure 27 overleaf** shows the number of local authorities which engaged with a range of other statutory agencies and voluntary and community organisations in the strategy making process. However the level of engagement of these bodies varied from full membership of a steering group to being asked simply to comment on a draft strategy.

3.38 By taking a more strategic approach to the management of homelessness in their area, many local authorities have specified clearer objectives and priorities for their voluntary and community sector partners. These have taken the form of Service Level Agreements in some areas. The objectives of both statutory and voluntary sectors are now better aligned in many areas.

Strategies have led to changes in approach

3.39 Ninety-seven per cent of authorities believe that formulating a strategy clarified their thinking on homelessness, and 78 per cent of voluntary, community and charitable groups agree **(Figure 28 overleaf)**.

CASE EXAMPLE 10

Multi-agency working in Carlisle

Carlisle's strategy making process involved a county-wide review of homelessness, covering six authorities in Cumbria. The strategy states explicitly that homelessness cannot be tackled in isolation and sets out how a partnership approach will be used to tackle and prevent homelessness in the county.

A Cumbria Homelessness Forum has been established which continues to meet each quarter to discuss homelessness issues in the county. It is a multi-agency forum comprising statutory and voluntary homelessness service providers from across Cumbria. These include:

Shelter (Chair)	NACRO Prison Service Plus
Citizens Advice Bureaux	Youth Offending Team
Cumbria Rural Housing Trust	Probation
Six different Housing Assocations (Two Castles, Eden, Impact, Carlisle, Derwent & Solway)	Cumbria Action for Social Support (housing advice and floating support for probation clients)
Community law centre	Cumbria Adolescents Resource Team
Digs (Deposit guarantee scheme)	Connexions
Hostel managers from across the region	Community mental health teams
Community Projects Carlisle	Cumbria County Council Social Services
Cumbria Supporting People	Stonham Housing Association (housing advice and support for ex-offenders)

The Forum's role includes promoting wider membership and monitoring the progress of each district's implementation plans.

Source: National Audit Office/Carlisle City Council

3.40 Our visits to local authorities and the Directorate's review of strategies both highlighted how, encouraged by the Directorate, many local authorities have used strategy making and accompanying funding to:

■ restructure their housing advice services **(Case Example 11)**;

■ place more weight on prevention of homelessness **(Case Example 12)**; and

■ build up new routes out of homelessness **(Case Example 13)**.

3.41 In reviewing services in the local area for the strategy, some authorities identified gaps in service provision. Many of these have been addressed by specially commissioned or extended services from the voluntary and community sector. In 2002-03, some 245 local authorities made grants of £21.4 million to voluntary and community sector organisations, an average of £87,000 per authority. By 2003-04, this had risen to £35.9 million distributed by 296 authorities, an average of £121,000 from each authority.[20]

---

20   HQNS (2004), *Evaluation of Local Authorities' Homelessness Strategies, ODPM.*

27 Local authorities consulted a wide range of organisations during the strategy making process

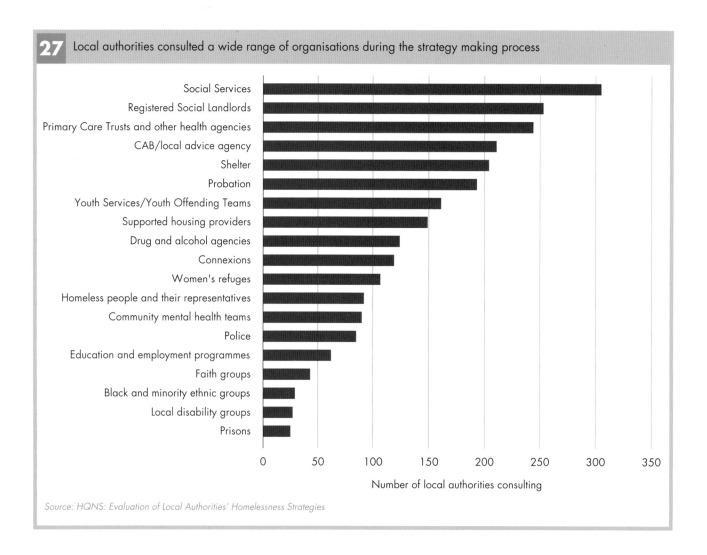

Source: HQNS: Evaluation of Local Authorities' Homelessness Strategies

28 Local authorities and the voluntary sector believe many positive benefits have derived from devising strategies

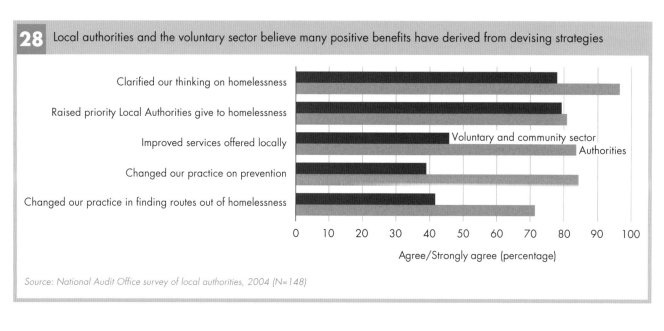

Source: National Audit Office survey of local authorities, 2004 (N=148)

CASE EXAMPLE 11

Changing the face of services in Hammersmith & Fulham - offering solutions, rather than processing applications

Before 2003, someone with housing difficulties approaching the Council would be seen by a Homelessness Officer – someone who judged the homeless person's situation against the criteria for statutory homelessness laid out in the law – for example, whether they were intentionally homeless, or in priority need. Homelessness Officers were the gatekeepers to social housing - their main focus was on assessing to whom the Council owed a legal duty. If the homeless person had support needs, they would be referred to a different department, and be assessed separately at another interview for extra assistance.

As part of the homelessness strategy development and implementation of the B&B target, the Directorate's special advisors helped Hammersmith & Fulham to restructure their services.

Now when a homeless or potentially homeless person contacts the borough, they first meet an 'Options' advisor for a discussion about how best to address their housing need, for example by helping them stay where they are, finding a home in the private sector, directing them to a rent deposit scheme, or where necessary, making a full homelessness application with a view to eventually receiving a council or RSL tenancy. The Supporting People team are part of the same divisional structure so homeless people with additional support needs can be identified at the same time and helped in a more co-ordinated way.

Source: National Audit Office

CASE EXAMPLE 12

Doncaster MBC introduces a new service: Homelessness Prevention Services

The drawing up of a homelessness strategy pushed prevention up the agenda for Councillors and Officers. The authority now has two dedicated officers - one with voluntary sector experience, the second with housing benefits experience - working solely on preventing homelessness.

Their promotional leaflet, widely distributed among landlords, Registered Social Landlords, government agencies and local voluntary groups sets out the range of housing issues which they will address:

- Rent arrears and payment arrangements
- Housing Benefit and Council Tax problems
- Eviction
- Debt
- Sign posting to other services or agencies
- Referrals to tenancy support
- Referrals to bond guarantee schemes
- Assistance with securing accommodation
- Access to mediation services
- Working with private sector landlords

Source: Doncaster MBC

CASE EXAMPLE 13

Routes out of homelessness – Brent's experimental approaches

Homefinders –many people approach Brent Council because they find it difficult to find somewhere to live in London, Brent has set up a free, online 'clearing house' for private sector tenancies. Potential tenants can browse the lists of properties which landlords advertise, and there are no fees for either party. The site receives half a million hits each year. To widen access, details of property vacancies are also displayed at all the Council's One-Stop Shops.

Save as you stay – Brent Council encourages ex-rough sleepers in short term accommodation to save a deposit for their next tenancy by matching the money they put aside.

Breaking the Chain – Brent Council will help homeless people find private rented accommodation on a two-year or longer lease. With agreement, their homelessness application is closed, and they are admitted to the main housing register. So far 200 households have taken this alternative to temporary accommodation.

Loft conversion scheme – Brent's homeless families tend to be larger than average. With few four and five bedroom houses in the borough, they could wait in temporary accommodation for years. By converting the lofts of existing properties into more bedrooms, Brent Council has been able to move 18 larger families out of temporary accommodation.

Source: National Audit Office

3.42 Four out of five local authorities believe that services to homeless people in their area have been improved as a result of the strategy making process. However, less than half of the voluntary and community bodies that we surveyed agreed (Figure 28).

The Directorate has identified a number of areas for further development in the strategies

3.43 All 354 local authorities in England conducted a review and produced a strategy by the end of July 2003, and most also generated an action plan. The quality of the documents varied widely. The main areas for further development identified in the assessment of strategies by the Directorate's independent consultants are outlined in **Figure 29 overleaf.**

3.44 Local authorities collect fairly basic information (using P1E forms) on the causes of homelessness. P1E is designed to monitor the decisions and actions of local authorities under the homelessness legislation, rather than to provide information on homeless households. Many local authorities identified this lack of information as a constraint on their ability to plan appropriately.

29 A number of areas of further development have been identified in the strategies

In the **reviews** of local homelessness upon which the strategy was based:

- Inability to obtain and analyse data on the full range of homelessness needs.

- Few evaluated the success or otherwise of existing services, especially prevention and tenancy support initiatives.

- Only one half of authorities fully considered **all** homeless people.

- Social Services often did not take part in the review.

- Significant participation by homelessness service users was rare.

- Only one in twelve authorities had consulted BME groups.

In the **strategies** themselves:

- The strategy documents did not commonly include strategic objectives. Some proposals were vague, and their objectives were unclear.

- One in five did not consider the needs of non-statutorily homeless people.

- Schemes were included despite inadequate evaluations of their usefulness.

- Authorities that did not use Bed & Breakfast tended not to consider how they would avoid doing so in the future. Some strategies stated that they would monitor Bed & Breakfast use but did not include actions to control it.

- Many authorities did not address rough sleeping in their plans. Where it was addressed, the strategies tended to focus on providing temporary accommodation.

In **action plans**:

- Monitoring and evaluation arrangements are weak.

- Few authorities have SMART (Specific, Measurable, Achievable, Revelant Time-related) targets. Hence, the monitoring of progress will be difficult.

- Ill defined responsibilities and timetables for actions.

- Four out of ten authorities failed to identify the resources they need to fulfil their strategy. Most did not consider the full range of funding opportunities.

Source: HQNS: Evaluation of Local Authorities' Homelessness Strategies

3.45 Although local authorities submitted their strategies by July 2003, they did not receive formal feedback until the Directorate had completed a review of strategies in Summer 2004. Due to the time lag in obtaining feedback, some local authorities completed an early review of progress without the benefit of being able to address identified areas for further development in their strategies.

More needs to be done to identify and spread good practice on what works cost-effectively

3.46 Three quarters of local authorities responding to our survey agreed that they now receive better assistance and advice in tackling homelessness than they did before the Directorate was created. Where the Directorate has been active, for example in promoting the lessons from Beacon Councils, this has been very well received by authorities **(Case Example 14)**.

3.47 Local authorities told us that the most important source of new ideas is their own staff **(Figure 30)**, although this was matched in importance by a combination of the Directorate's outputs – presentations, discussions and publications. Staff may generate solutions tailored to local circumstances. The Directorate's independent review of strategies showed that few local authorities had been able to evaluate the success or otherwise of their existing services and initiatives, although many of these were fairly new. Local authorities identified a need for evidence-based guidance on what works if they are to achieve positive changes in their homelessness services.

CASE EXAMPLE 14

Spreading the word – West Wiltshire and the Beacon Councils

In 2003, West Wiltshire's homelessness unit, with the support of the Directorate, visited Leicester, Colchester and Harrow Councils - Beacon councils tackling homelessness.

Twelve staff attended and came back enthused, with a list of new ideas, and a desire to transfer the lessons for West Wiltshire.

As a result, the nature and range of services on offer to homeless people in the District has changed – they now have staff trained in debt counselling and building links with private sector landlords. The unit has switched from processing homelessness applications, to providing genuine options. Staff in the unit are proud that they have adapted the Beacons' ideas and delivered real achievements, for example, eliminating the use of Bed & Breakfast for homeless families.

Source: National Audit Office

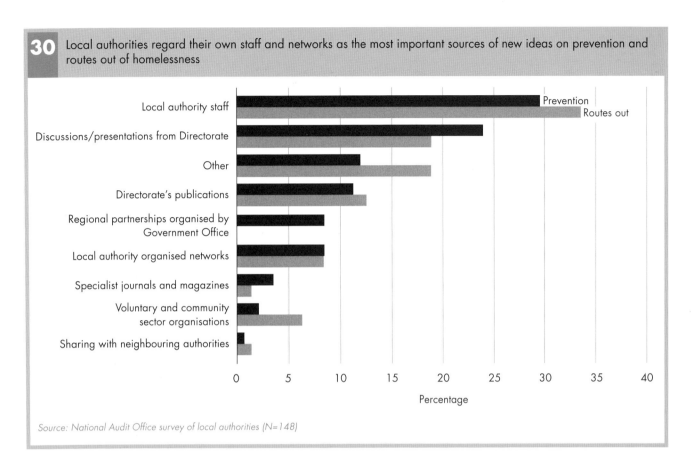

30 Local authorities regard their own staff and networks as the most important sources of new ideas on prevention and routes out of homelessness

Source: National Audit Office survey of local authorities (N=148)

The Directorate has commissioned an assessment of a number of preventative services and initiatives in order to identify successful approaches and good practice. This is due to report early in 2005.

The Directorate should consider clarifying the role of Government Offices in tackling homelessness

3.48 The nine regional Government Offices have a potentially important role in ensuring local homelessness strategies and approaches reflect regional issues. A Government Office representative sits on each of the nine Regional Housing Boards. Regional Housing Boards were established in 2003 to strengthen the integration of the various strategic and planning processes and to co-ordinate the arrangements for establishing regional housing priorities (covering both targeting of housing expenditure and other action to improve delivery or service performance). The Board is also responsible for making recommendations to Ministers on how the overall resources available for the region through local authorities and Registered Social Landlords should be allocated. Regional Housing Boards are expected to consider homelessness issues in devising regional housing strategies.

3.49 The Directorate has encouraged all Government Offices to consider how they can help the achievement of homelessness objectives in the regions and has offered funding for regional and sub-regional initiatives, but has not formally set down its expectations of the Government Offices in tackling homelessness. We found a variety of approaches in the Government Offices we visited. Some saw their role as acting as a conduit between local authorities and the Directorate and took a pro-active role in developing co-ordinated approaches to identifying regional issues. For example, Government Office Yorkshire & the Humber organise and host road shows to develop communication networks and offer guidance and consultation over strategies, funding bids and local circumstances. Others were uncomfortable with being regarded as a source of expert advice and opportunities such as spreading best practice were approached in an ad hoc manner. There is, therefore, clear potential to make the contribution of the Government Offices more consistent and effective.

APPENDIX A

Our methodology

1   We adopted a variety of methods in our examination of homelessness. The methods were chosen in order to:

■   measure progress against targets;

■   explore the progress local authorities and the voluntary and community sector have made in tackling homelessness;

■   canvass the views of service providers;

■   hear the voice of the homeless people.

2   The main methods that we adopted were:

Secondary data analysis

3   We examined several forms of secondary evidence to broaden our knowledge and understanding of the subject area:

■   ODPM research, policy documents relating to target setting, evidence of partnership working with other government departments and quarterly statistical releases to show trends and distribution of homelessness.

■   Literature reviews, including information from the Audit Commission, Crisis, Shelter, the National Centre for Social Research, and the Barker Review: Delivering Stability: Securing Our Future Housing Needs, 2004.

■   Statistical data from the Greater London Authority and the Chartered Institute of Public Finance and Accountancy.

■   To put the English approach into context, we reviewed the approach to homelessness taken by other parts of the United Kingdom.

Postal survey of providers

4   We conducted separate postal surveys of local authorities and the voluntary and community sector between June and August 2004. They were designed to obtain statistical data, evidence of activities undertaken to tackle homelessness, and information on the progress of the Directorate and its targets. We targeted all 354 housing authorities, and identified around 450 voluntary and community sector groups (a mixture of day centres, hostels, resettlement services and drug and alcohol services) from the mailing list of Homeless Link, a national membership organisation for homeless agencies. We had responses from 145 local authorities and 59 voluntary and community sector groups.

Visits to local authorities

5   We visited six case study local authorities between late May and August 2004 to gain in depth information relating to local strategies, financial costs, difficulties encountered, awareness of regional differences and relationships with the Directorate. We chose these authorities to provide a broad geographical spread, and to cover urban and rural areas that had a significant homeless population. The authorities visited are shown in the annex to the Executive Summary.

6   We conducted interviews with personnel including accommodation, housing and homelessness officers, directors of strategy and partnership, and housing services managers. Where appropriate we also met the local authority's strategic partners and visited units of temporary accommodation.

Consultation with central government bodies

7   We conducted interviews with other central government bodies between May and September 2004, to determine the level of collaboration with ODPM in tackling homelessness. These bodies included:

■   Department for Education and Skills

■   Department of Health

■   Department for Work and Pensions

■   HM Prison Service

■   Home Office

■   National Asylum Support Service

Consultation with the voluntary and community sector and other stakeholders

8 Throughout the preparation and planning for this examination, and during the fieldwork stages, we consulted widely with key interest groups and stakeholders. These groups included:

- Action on Homelessness
- Amber Project
- Association of London Government
- Audit Commission
- Broadway
- Centre for Housing Policy, University of York
- Centrepoint
- Chartered Institute for Housing
- Crisis
- European Federation of National Organisations Working with the Homeless (FEANTSA)
- Government Offices – South West, North West, Yorkshire & the Humber
- Homeless Link
- Joint Centre for Scottish Housing Research
- Joseph Rowntree Foundation
- Outreach workers from mental health services and prisons
- National Housing Federation
- National Rent Deposit Forum
- Registered Social Landlords
- Scottish Council for Single Homeless
- Scottish Executive
- Shelter
- St. Mungo's
- Threshold

Expert panel

9 We organised an expert panel to comment on our methodological approach and preliminary findings. Members of the panel were:

- Robert Aldridge – Director, Scottish Centre for Single Homeless
- Martin Cheeseman – Director of Housing, Brent Borough Council
- Professor Suzanne Fitzpatrick – Centre for Housing Policy, University of York
- Gill Green – Senior Manager, Housing, Communities and Environment, Audit Commission
- Helen Lewis – Policy Officer, Shelter
- Geoffrey Randall – Consultant, Research and Information Services
- Mike Atherton – Head of Housing and Consumer Services, Telford and Wrekin Unitary Authority

Discussion with homeless people

10 We commissioned IFF Research Ltd to conduct research with the homeless in our case study areas. They carried out this work in July and August 2004. The information gathered provided evidence on the strengths and weaknesses of homeless services, the quality of accommodation, and relationships with providers. IFF Research ran interviews and group discussions involving 59 individuals, including:

- current rough sleepers;
- those that have slept rough but have now found some sort of accommodation; and
- former long-term users of Bed & Breakfast accommodation

APPENDIX B

Tackling homelessness in other parts of the United Kingdom

Scotland   Number of Households: 2,220,000

Homelessness Statistics

Year	Applications	Assessed as Homeless	Assessed as Homeless & in Priority Need	Number per thousand household
2001-02	47,493	37,100	26,900	12.12
2002-03	51,738	38,446	28,177	12.69
2003-04	54,829	38,659	28,168	12.69

Temporary Accommodation

	TOTAL	B&B	LA Stock/Hostel	Other
as at 31st March 2002	4,153	569	3,515	69
as at 31st March 2003	5,488	914	4,433	141
as at 31st March 2004	6,574	1,206	5,236	132

Scale of homelessness

The number of homeless applications has increased from 47,493 applications in 2001-02 to 54,829 applications in 2003-04, a rise of 15%. The number assessed as homeless and in priority need has increased over the same period from 26,900 in 2001-02, to 28,168, a rise of 4.7%.

The number of households placed in temporary accommodation by local authorities has risen from 4,153 as at 31 March 2002 to 6,574 as at 31 March 2004. Use of Bed & Breakfast accommodation has more than doubled from 569 in 2002 to 1,206 in 2004. As at 31 March 2004, there were 151 households with children in Bed & Breakfast accommodation.

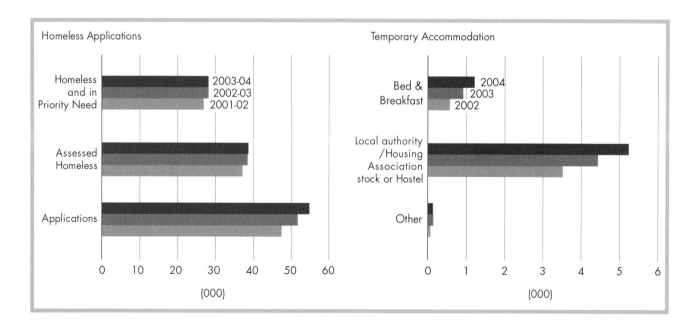

Responsibilities

The Scottish Executive is responsible for overall policy and legislation. Responsibility for front-line delivery of services to the homeless rests with local authorities.

Developments

In 1999 the Scottish Executive set up a Homelessness Task Force to 'review the causes and nature of homelessness and to examine current practice in Scotland'. Recommendations of the task force resulted in two new pieces of legislation:

The Housing (Scotland) Act 2001 which introduced a number of new duties:

- All people in priority need and unintentionally homeless now have the right to permanent accommodation

- All people who present as homeless have the right to temporary accommodation until their application is resolved.

- Every local authority had to produce a strategy to prevent and alleviate homelessness in its area;

- Local authorities' homelessness functions became subject to regulation and inspection by Communities Scotland;

- New regulations setting out rights and responsibilities of residents in, and providers of, hostels and other forms of insecure accommodation are currently being consulted on and will come into force late on this year.

The Homelessness (Scotland) Act 2003, has so far been implemented in part. The following came into force in December 2004;

- New regulation requiring temporary accommodation for households with children or pregnant women to meet minimum standards in all but exceptional circumstances.

The 2003 Act sets the framework to extend the rights of homeless people still further. It allows Scottish Ministers to abolish the test of priority need and incorporates a target for abolition of 2012. At that point, all unintentionally homeless people will have the right to permanent accommodation. Ministers also have the power to modify current local connection rules. Work is currently being carried out to assess in more detail the potential implications of these changes for each local authority.

The 2003 Act will also require those found to be intentionally homeless to be provided with a short tenancy and support.

The Scottish Health Boards are also required to implement Health & Homelessness Action Plans in partnership with the local authority or authorities in their area to ensure that the health needs of homeless people are being met.

The statutory code of Guidance which Local Authorities must have regard of when carrying out homelessness duties is currently being updated and will be published this Spring. Major changes reflect the new regulations on temporary accommodation, and an updated chapter on people subject to immigration control.

Sources: Scottish Executive Statistical Bulletin August 2004, Scottish Executive Website, Scottish Council for Single Homeless

Wales				Number of Households: 1,210,000

Homelessness Statistics

Year	Applications	Assessed as Homeless	Assessed as Homeless & in Priority Need	Number per thousand household
2001-02	13,982	3,965	5,333	4.41
2002-03	17,030	4,609	6,965	5.76
2003-04	20,935	5,369	9,147	7.56

Temporary Accommodation

	TOTAL	B&B	LA Stock/Hostel	Other
as at 31st March 2002	877	123	535	219
as at 31st March 2003	1272	302	631	339
as at 31st March 2004	1759	691	576	492

Scale of homelessness

The number of homeless applications has increased from 13,982 applications in 2001-02 to 20,935 applications in 2003-04, a rise of almost 50%. The number assessed as homeless and in priority need over the same period has increased from 5,333 in 2001-02, to 9,147, a rise of almost 70%,

Use of temporary accommodation increased from 877 as at 31 March 2002 to 1,759 as at 31 March 2004. Use of Bed & Breakfast accommodation has increased by more than 5 times from 123 in 2002 to 691 in 2004.

There were 2,900 households in temporary accommodation at the end of March 2004. There were 691 households in Bed & Breakfast accommodation, of which167 were families with children.

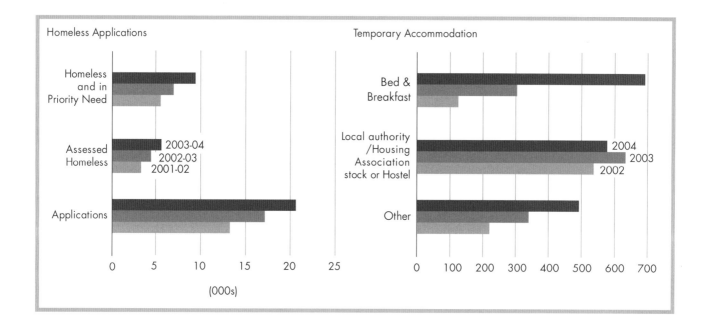

Responsibilities

The Welsh Assembly is responsible for overall policy with some secondary legislation powers. Responsibility for front-line delivery of services to the homeless rests with local authorities. Responsibility for primary legislation rests with the UK government. This includes the Housing Act 1996 and the Homelessness Act 2002, which incorporate the main duties on local authorities, and which apply to Wales.

In November 2000 a Homelessness Commission was set up to advise the Assembly on reducing homelessness, including rough sleeping. Following the report of the Commission, the Welsh Assembly Government adopted a National Homelessness Strategy and Action Plan in April 2003.

Developments

The Welsh Assembly Government has revised its statutory Code of Guidance for local authorities on Allocation and Homelessness to reflect the changes in the Homelessness Act 2002, and is revising the Regulatory Code for Registered Social Landlords to reflect their strategic responsibilities in this area. The Welsh Assembly has assessed all local authority homelessness reviews and strategies and provided advice on how they should be strengthened.

Progress on the National Homelessness Strategy for Wales is monitored by an advisory group, the Homelessness Strategies Review Group. A full review of the Strategy began in October 2004, involving wide consultation with different sectors and interests. This review will conclude in March 2005, and a revised Strategy will be issued soon after.

In October 2002 the Welsh Assembly Government commissioned HACAS Chapman Hendy to review the implementation of homelessness legislation in Wales. The report found a range of problems with the implementation of the legislation, including how local authorities were using Bed & Breakfast and out-of-borough accommodation to meet the demand for temporary accommodation. The Welsh Assembly has announced its intention to introduce legislation to restrict the use of Bed & Breakfast establishments for families and young people, and detailed proposals will be issued for consultation during 2005. Other recommendations will be addressed through the review of the National Homelessness Strategy.

The Assembly provides a Homelessness and Rooflessness grant programme in Wales.

Welsh Housing Statistics show that the introduction of the extra priority need categories in March 2001 led to an increase in both applications and acceptances of around 1,000 cases in 2001-02. The majority of the increase in homelessness since then appears to be due to wider market trends.

Sources: Statistical Bulletin Homelessness in Wales: 2002-03, The Welsh Assembly

Northern Ireland

Number of Households: 650,000

Homelessness Statistics

Year	Applications	Full Duty Applicant	Number per thousand household
2001-02	12,694	6,500	10.00
2002-03	16,426	8,580	13.20
2003-04	17,150	8,594	13.22

Temporary Accommodation

	TOTAL	B&B	LA Stock/Hostel	Other
as at 31st March 2002	Not available	Not available	Not available	Not available
as at 31st March 2003	Not available	Not available	Not available	Not available
as at 31st March 2004	923	132	175	336

Scale of homelessness

Those who apply to the Northern Ireland Housing Executive as homeless are assessed on whether they meet the legal criteria i.e. are 'unintentionally homeless' and in 'priority need'. Those who meet the legal criteria are referred to as Full Duty applicants. In 2003-04 8,594 (50 per cent) were Full Duty applicants – and received the full level of assistance available under the law.

The number of homeless applications has increased from 12,694 applications in 2001-02 to 17,150 applications in 2003-04, a rise of 26%. The number of Full Duty applicants has increased from 6,500 in 2001-02 to 8,594 in 2003-04, a rise of 24%. The number of Full Duty applicants per thousand household has increased from 10 in 2001-02 to13.22 in 2003-04.

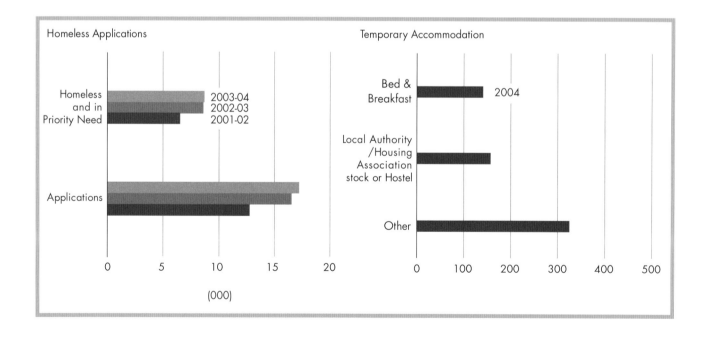

Responsibilities

The Housing Executive, a Non-Departmental Public Body, is responsible for tackling homelessness in Northern Ireland. Statutory responsibility for homelessness in Northern Ireland is governed by the 'Housing (NI) Order 1988'.

Developments

Throughout the 1990s the priority was to increase the supply of temporary accommodation. In 1988 there were only three hostels available for temporary accommodation. By March 2004 the Housing Executive had delivered 25 homeless hostels and was providing funding for a further 50 in the voluntary sector. It had also secured the use of some 200 units of private sector, self-contained accommodation.

In March 2002 the Northern Ireland Audit Office report 'Housing the Homeless' was published. The key findings of the subsequent Public Accounts Committee hearing were:

- Planning and provision of homelessness services had been inadequate and the Housing Executive took 14 years to develop a formal homeless strategy

- Although the Executive acknowledged the unsuitability of Bed & Breakfast accommodation it used this accommodation for over half of its homeless clients in 2000-01 at an estimated cost of £7.5 million

- Length of stay in Bed & Breakfast accommodation was three times longer than an informal target of 33 days.

In September 2002 the Housing Executive published the Northern Ireland Homelessness Strategy focusing on preventing homelessness and providing support. Similar targets to England were set.

By the end of March 2004 there were no homeless families with children in Bed & Breakfast accommodation longer than six weeks and the Executive has a target to cease the use of Bed & Breakfast accommodation for all households (except in emergencies) by April 2006.

Sources: The Housing Executive Website, PAC Report May 2004, NI Audit Office Report March 2002, DSD Northern Ireland Housing Bulletin, 1 January – 31 March 2004, NI Labour Force Survey 1997-2002

REPORTS BY THE COMPTROLLER AND AUDITOR GENERAL, SESSION 2004-2005

The Comptroller and Auditor General has to date, in Session 2004-2005, presented to the House of Commons the following reports under Section 9 of the National Audit Act, 1983. The reports are listed by subject category.

		Publication date
Agriculture		
Foot and Mouth Disease: Applying the Lessons	HC 184	2 February 2005
Cross-Government Reports		
Delivering Public Services to a Diverse Society - Report	HC 19 - I	10 December 2004
- Case Studies	HC 19 - II	10 December 2004
Culture, Media and Sport		
UK Sport: Supporting elite athletes	HC 182 SE/2005/9	27 January 2005
Education		
Improving school attendance in England	HC 212	4 February 2005
Skills for Life: Improving adult literacy and numeracy	HC 20	15 December 2004
English Regions		
More than a roof: Progress in tackling homelessness	HC 286	23 February 2005
Law, Order and Central		
Reducing Crime: The Home Office Working with Crime and Disorder Reduction Partnerships	HC 16	1 December 2004
Home Office - Reducing Vehicle Crime	HC 183	28 January 2005
National Health Service		
Patient Choice at the Point of GP Referral	HC 180	19 January 2005
Reforming NHS Dentistry: Ensuring effective management of risks	HC 25	25 November 2004
Darent Valley Hospital: The PFI Contract in Action	HC 209	10 February 2005
Public Private Partnership		
English Partnerships: Regeneration of the Millennium Dome and Associated Land	HC 178	12 January 2005
Revenue departments		
Inland Revenue: Inheritance Tax	HC 17	3 December 2004
HM Customs and Excise: Gambling Duties	HC 188	14 January 2005
Trade and Industry		
Renewable Energy	HC 210	11 February 2005

		Publication date
Transport		
Tackling congestion by making better use of England's motorways and trunk roads	HC 15	26 November 2004
Work and Pensions		
Managing Attendance in the Department for Work and Pensions	HC 18	8 December 2004
Helping those in financial hardship: the running of the Social Fund	HC 179	13 January 2005
Transfer of property to the private sector under the expansion of the PRIME Contract	HC 181	26 January 2005

Printed in the UK for the Stationery Office Limited
on behalf of the Controller of her Majesty's Stationery Office
176723   02/05   65536